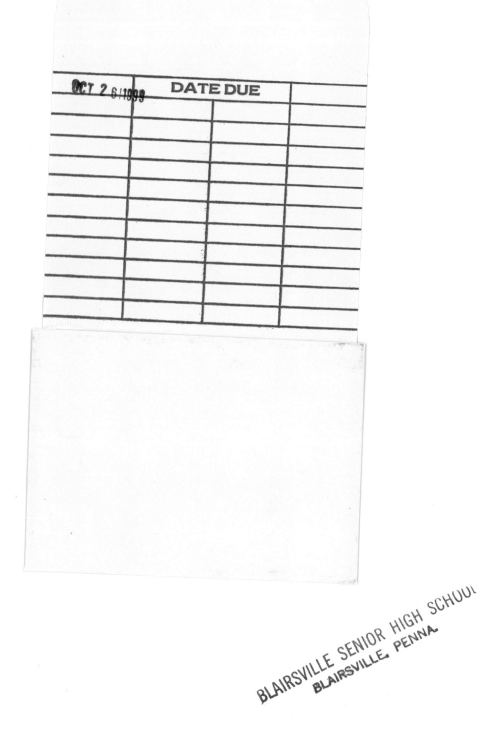

Using and Understanding Maps

The Economy of the World

Consulting Editor

Scott E. Morris

College of Mines and Earth Resources
University of Idaho

Chelsea House Publishers
New York   Philadelphia

This Publication was designed, edited and computer generated by
Lovell Johns Limited
10 Hanborough Business Park
Long Hanborough
Witney
Oxon, England OX8 8LH

General Editor and Project Manager   Alison Dickinson
Research and Text   Gill Lloyd

The contents of this volume are based on the latest data available at the
time of publication.

Map credit: *Antarctica source map prepared at 1:20,000 by the British
Antarctic Survey Mapping and Geographic Information Centre, 1990.*

Cover credit: *Robert Frerck/Woodfin Camp and Associates.*

Printed in Mexico

3 5 7 9 8 6 4 2

Library of Congress Cataloging in Publication Data

The Economy of the world/editorial consultant, Scott Morris:
        p. cm.—(Using and understanding maps)
        Includes glossary and index/gazetteer.
        Includes bibliographical references.
        Summary: Eighteen map spreads, charts, and diagrams explain the
        economy of the world.
        ISBN 0-7910-1809-1. — ISBN 0-7910-1822-9 (pbk.)
        1. Econopmic geography—Maps. 2. International trade—Maps.
        [1. Economic geography—Maps, 2. Atlases.]
        I. Morris, Scott Edward. II. Chelsea House Publishers. III Series.
        G1046.G1E38 1993 <G&M>
        330.9' .0022' 3 — dc20   92-22291
                                                        CIP
                                                        MAP AC

Introduction

We inhabit a fascinating and mysterious planet where the earth's physical features, life-forms, and the diversity of human culture conspire to produce a breathtaking environment. We don't have to travel very far to see and experience the wealth of this diverse planet; in fact, we don't have to travel at all. Everywhere images of the world are abundantly available in books, newspapers, magazines, movies, television, and the arts. We could say that *everywhere* one looks, our world is a brilliant moving tapestry of shapes, colors, and textures, and our experience of its many messages — whether in our travels or simply by gazing out into our own backyards — is what we call reality.

Geography is the study of a portion of that reality. More so, it is the study of how the physical and biological components (rocks, animals, plants, and people) of our planet are distributed and how they are interconnected. Geographers seek to describe and to explain the physical patterns that have evolved on the earth and also to discover the significance in the ways they have evolved. To do this, geographers rely on maps.

Maps can be powerful images. They convey selective information about vast areas of an overwhelmingly cluttered world. The cartographer, or mapmaker, must carefully choose the theme of a map, that is, what it will show, knowing that a good map will convey the essence of information while at the same time making the information easy to comprehend.

This volume and its companions in UNDERSTANDING AND USING MAPS are about the planet we call earth and the maps we use to find our way along its peaks and valleys. Each volume displays map images that reveal how the world is arranged according to a specific theme such as population, industries or the endangered world. The maps in each volume are accompanied by an interesting collection of facts — some are rather obvious, others are oddities. Yet all are meant to be informative.

Along with a wealth of facts, there are explanations of the various attributes and phenomena depicted by the maps. This information is provided to better understand the significance of the maps as well as to demonstrate how the many themes relate.

Names for places are essential to geographers. To study the world without devising names for places would be extremely difficult. But geographers also know that names are in no way permanent; place names change as people change. The recent reunification of Germany and the breakup of what was the Soviet Union — events that seem colossal from the perspective of socioeconomics — to geographers are simply events that require the drawing or erasing of one or a few boundaries and the renaming of one or several land masses. The geographer is constantly reminded that the world is in flux; a map is always in danger of being rendered obsolete by a turn in current events.

Because the world is dynamic, it continues to captivate the mind and stimulate the imagination. USING AND UNDERSTANDING MAPS presents the world as it is today, with the reservation that any dramatic rearrangement of land and people is likely, indeed inevitable, thus requiring the making of a new map. In this way maps are themselves a part of the evolutionary process.

Scott E. Morris

The Economy of the World

At first glance, economics seems quite simple — one person produces something and sells it to another. But when this simple business transaction is multiplied a billion times to encompass all of the raw materials and finished goods and services circulating throughout the entire world, and when billions of people speaking different languages and using different money engage in trade, you can begin to appreciate how complicated economics really is.

There are three major types of economies: subsistence, free-market, and planned. As the name suggests, subsistence economies are those in which a limited number of simple goods and services are produced and consumed by the producers and their local communities. Goods are traded for other goods, and money may not be used at all. Human beings started out as hunters and gatherers in a subsistence economy, and a few primitive peoples practice this system even today. Free-market or commercial economies are the most common in the world today. In this system, producers make commodities, goods created strictly for sale in marketplaces rather than for immediate or local use. The value of these goods is determined by supply and demand, and competition serves as a restraint on producers who wish to raise prices. Most often, free-market economies require a universally accepted currency to make buying and selling easier, but trading and bartering also take place. Planned economies are those in which a central agency, usually a government, decides what is produced, how much is produced, and how much products should sell for. This central agency often owns nation's farms, industries, and transportation network.

No economy is "pure," however. For example, the United States is often used as a prime example of a free-market economy, yet the government regulates many economic activities, and the laws of supply and demand and competition do not always apply. Likewise, the planned economies of the former socialist states of eastern Europe always possessed a healthy, commercial "black market" and are now moving quite rapidly to develop the mechanisms of a free-market economy. And even in the poorest subsistence economies, surplus goods are sold or traded in a local market.

Although the economy of a single country might seem quite complex, with manufacturing and service industries of various kinds concentrated within different regions, there is only one currency to contend with and, usually, a consistent set of rules for buying and selling. International economics is far more complicated. In the modern world, money, goods, and services flow in all directions. Modern transportation networks allow people to move products cheaply across town or across the ocean. From basic raw material such as crude oil, aluminum, steel, and timber to sophisticated electronic equipment, millions of purchases take place every day. Even money itself is bought and sold.

The long-term economic health of a country is dependent on its balance of payments, the relationship between what it buys and imports from other countries and what it sells and exports to other countries. A trade surplus is generally preferable; that is, countries want to receive more money from exports than they spend on imports. Currently, many of the less developed countries (LDCs) in Latin America and Africa are in economic trouble. Not only are they running trade deficits, that is, buying more foreign goods than they can pay for by selling their own products abroad, but they have borrowed heavily from developed countries and are having difficulty paying off these debts. All is not well in developed countries either. The United States currently runs an enormous trade deficit. In 1987, this deficit amounted to more than $150 billion. This seems like an enormous amount of money, but it is really a paltry sum compared to the size of the gross national product (GNP) of the United States, which is more than $4 trillion a year! All the same, this trade deficit is a disturbing sign that many U.S. products are losing their appeal to both foreign and domestic consumers.

Scott E. Morris

A legend lists and explains the symbols and colors used on the map. It is called a legend because it tells the story of a map. It is important to read the map legend to find out exactly what the symbols mean because some symbols do not look like what they represent. For example, a dot stands for a town.
Every map in this atlas has a legend on it.

This legend lists and explains the colors and symbols used on the map on that page only. The legend on the left, below, shows examples of the colors used on the maps in all the atlases in this series. Below this is a list of all symbols used on the maps in all the atlases in this series.
The legend on the right, below, is an example of a legend used in the physical atlas.

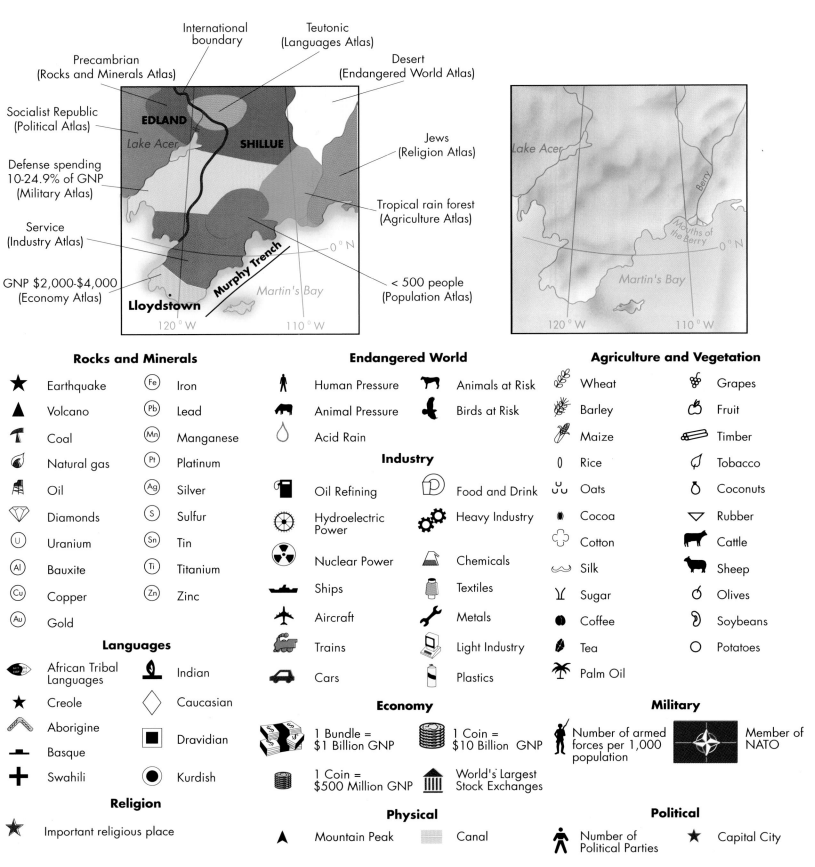

Rocks and Minerals

- ★ Earthquake
- ▲ Volcano
- ⊤ Coal
- Natural gas
- Oil
- ▽ Diamonds
- Ⓤ Uranium
- Ⓐⅼ Bauxite
- Ⓒᵤ Copper
- Ⓐᵤ Gold
- Ⓕₑ Iron
- Ⓟᵦ Lead
- Ⓜₙ Manganese
- Ⓟₜ Platinum
- Ⓐg Silver
- Ⓢ Sulfur
- Ⓢₙ Tin
- Ⓣᵢ Titanium
- Ⓩₙ Zinc

Languages

- African Tribal Languages
- ★ Creole
- Aborigine
- Basque
- ✚ Swahili
- Indian
- ◇ Caucasian
- ■ Dravidian
- ● Kurdish

Religion

- ★ Important religious place

Endangered World

- Human Pressure
- Animal Pressure
- Acid Rain
- Animals at Risk
- Birds at Risk

Industry

- Oil Refining
- Hydroelectric Power
- Nuclear Power
- Ships
- Aircraft
- Trains
- Cars
- Food and Drink
- Heavy Industry
- Chemicals
- Textiles
- Metals
- Light Industry
- Plastics

Economy

- 1 Bundle = $1 Billion GNP
- 1 Coin = $500 Million GNP
- 1 Coin = $10 Billion GNP
- World's Largest Stock Exchanges

Physical

- ▲ Mountain Peak
- Canal

Agriculture and Vegetation

- Wheat
- Barley
- Maize
- 0 Rice
- Oats
- Cocoa
- Cotton
- Silk
- Sugar
- Coffee
- Tea
- Palm Oil
- Grapes
- Fruit
- Timber
- Tobacco
- Coconuts
- ▽ Rubber
- Cattle
- Sheep
- Olives
- Soybeans
- O Potatoes

Military

- Number of armed forces per 1,000 population
- Member of NATO

Political

- Number of Political Parties
- ★ Capital City

World Physical

This page is a physical map of the world. It indicates where the major physical features — such as mountain ranges, plains, deserts, lakes, and rivers — are in the world. As the world is very large, the map has to be drawn at a very small scale in order to fit onto a page. This map is drawn at a scale so that 1 inch on the map, at the equator, equals 1,840 miles on the ground.

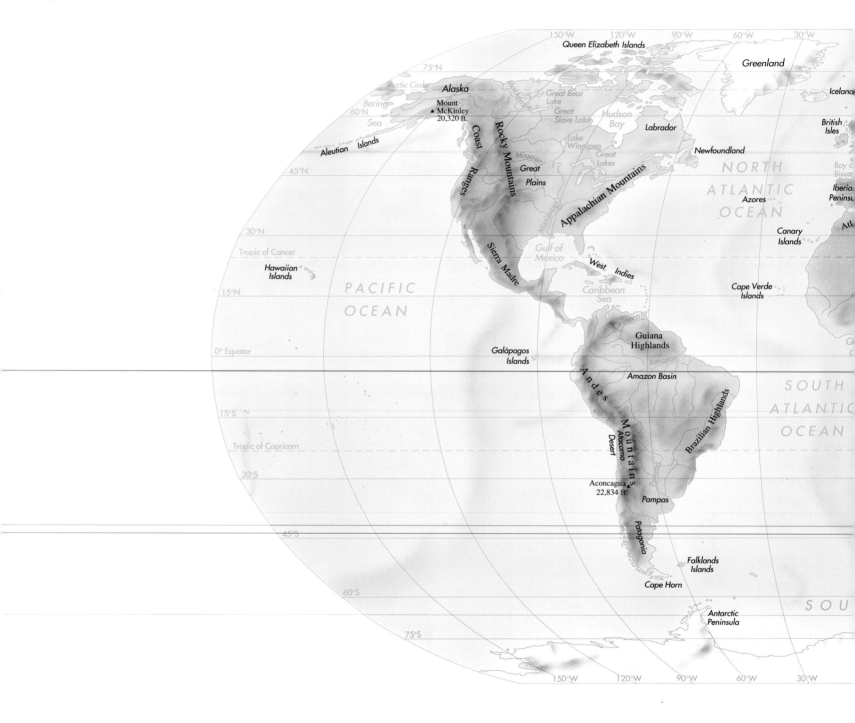

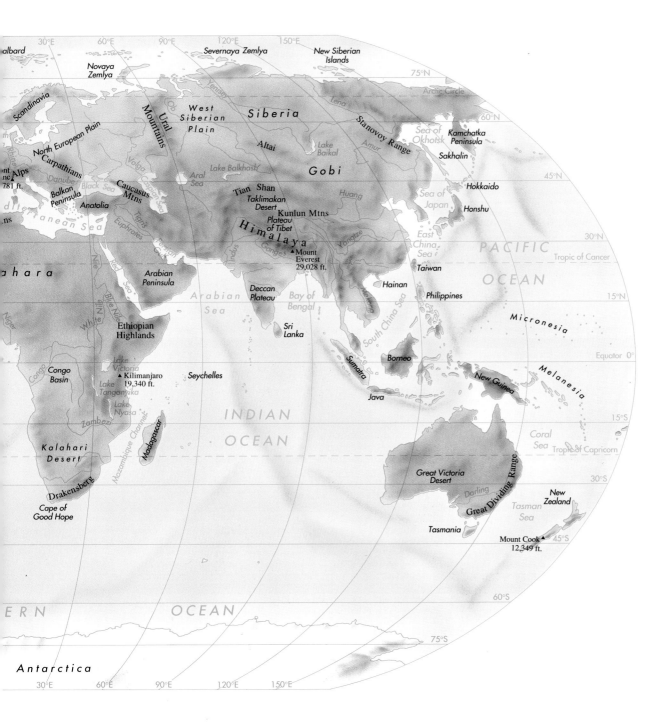

Svalbard

Novaya
Zemlya

Severnaya Zemlya

New Siberian
Islands

75°N

Arctic Circle

Scandinavia

West
Siberian
Plain

Siberia

Ural
Mountains

Stanovoy Range

Sea of
Okhotsk

Kamchatka
Peninsula

60°N

Yenisey

Lena

North European Plain

Amur

Altai

Lake
Baikal

Volga

Sakhalin

Carpathians

Danube

Caspian Sea

Lake Balkhash

Gobi

45°N

Alps

Black Sea

Aral
Sea

Sea of
Japan

Hokkaido

781 ft.

Caucasus
Mtns

Tian Shan

Huang

Balkan
Peninsula

Anatolia

Taklimakan
Desert

Honshu

Mediterranean Sea

Euphrates

Kunlun Mtns
Plateau
of Tibet

30°N

Himalaya

Yangtze

East
China
Sea

PACIFIC

Ganges

Indus

Sahara

Nile

Red Sea

Arabian
Peninsula

▲ Mount
Everest
29,028 ft.

Taiwan

OCEAN

Tropic of Cancer

Blue Nile

Deccan
Plateau

Hainan

Niger

White Nile

Arabian
Sea

Bay of
Bengal

Philippines

15°N

Sri
Lanka

South China Sea

Micronesia

Ethiopian
Highlands

Seychelles

Mekong

Equator 0°

Congo
Basin

Lake
Victoria

▲ Kilimanjaro
19,340 ft.

Sumatra

Borneo

New Guinea

Melanesia

Congo

Lake
Tanganyika

Java

15°S

Lake
Nyasa

Zambezi

INDIAN

Coral
Sea

Kalahari
Desert

Mozambique Channel

Madagascar

OCEAN

Tropic of Capricorn

Great Victoria
Desert

Great Dividing Range

30°S

Drakensberg

Darling

New
Zealand

Cape of
Good Hope

Tasman
Sea

Tasmania

Mount Cook ▲
12,349 ft.

45°S

60°S

ERN

OCEAN

75°S

Antarctica

30°E   60°E   90°E   120°E   150°E

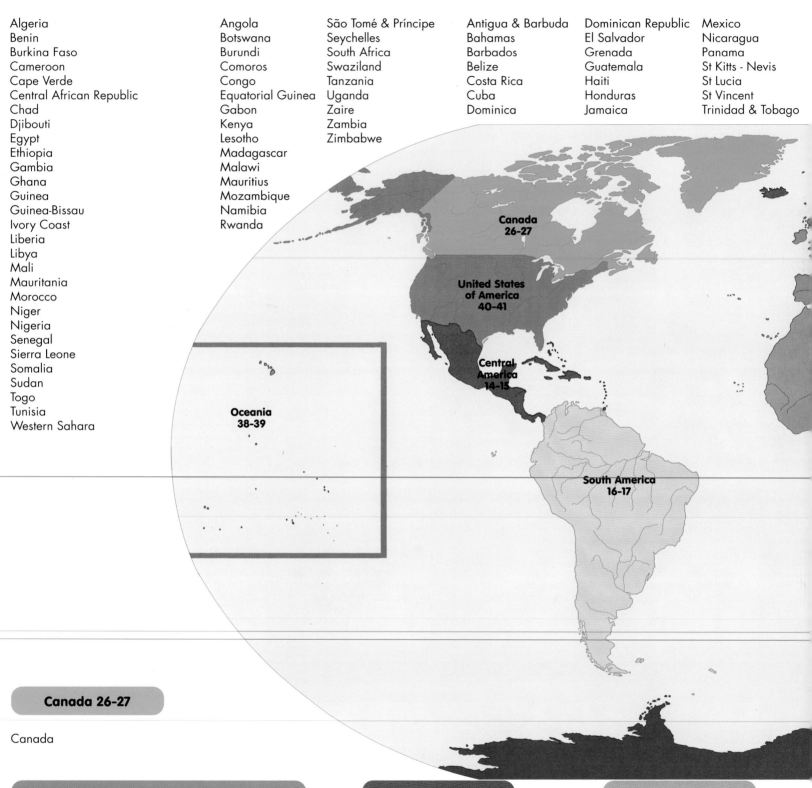

Africa, Northern 10-11

Algeria
Benin
Burkina Faso
Cameroon
Cape Verde
Central African Republic
Chad
Djibouti
Egypt
Ethiopia
Gambia
Ghana
Guinea
Guinea-Bissau
Ivory Coast
Liberia
Libya
Mali
Mauritania
Morocco
Niger
Nigeria
Senegal
Sierra Leone
Somalia
Sudan
Togo
Tunisia
Western Sahara

Africa, Southern 12-13

Angola
Botswana
Burundi
Comoros
Congo
Equatorial Guinea
Gabon
Kenya
Lesotho
Madagascar
Malawi
Mauritius
Mozambique
Namibia
Rwanda

São Tomé & Príncipe
Seychelles
South Africa
Swaziland
Tanzania
Uganda
Zaire
Zambia
Zimbabwe

America, Central 14-15

Antigua & Barbuda
Bahamas
Barbados
Belize
Costa Rica
Cuba
Dominica

Dominican Republic
El Salvador
Grenada
Guatemala
Haiti
Honduras
Jamaica

Mexico
Nicaragua
Panama
St Kitts - Nevis
St Lucia
St Vincent
Trinidad & Tobago

Canada 26-27

Canada

Commonwealth of Independent States 28-29

Armenia
Azerbaijan
Estonia
Georgia
Kazakhstan
Kirghizstan
Latvia
Lithuania
Moldova
Russian Federation

Tajikistan
Turkmenistan
Ukraine
Uzbekhistan

Europe 30-31

Albania
Bosnia & Herzegovina
Bulgaria
Croatia
Czechoslovakia
Finland
Greece
Hungary
Iceland
Norway

Poland
Romania
Slovenia
Sweden
Yugoslavia

Europe, Western 32-33

Andorra
Austria
Belgium
Denmark
France
Germany
Ireland
Italy
Liechtenstein
Luxembourg

Malta
Monaco
Netherlands
Portugal
San Marino
Spain
Switzerland
United Kingdom
Vatican City

America, South 16-17

Argentina	Guyana
Bolivia	Paraguay
Brazil	Peru
Chile	Suriname
Colombia	Uruguay
Ecuador	Venezuela
French Guiana	

Antarctica 18-19

Antarctica

Asia, East 20-21

China
Japan
Korea, North
Korea, South
Mongolia
Taiwan

Asia, Southeast 22-23

Brunei
Burma
Cambodia
Indonesia
Laos
Malaysia
Philippines
Singapore
Thailand
Vietnam

Australasia 24-25

Australia
New Zealand
Papua New Guinea

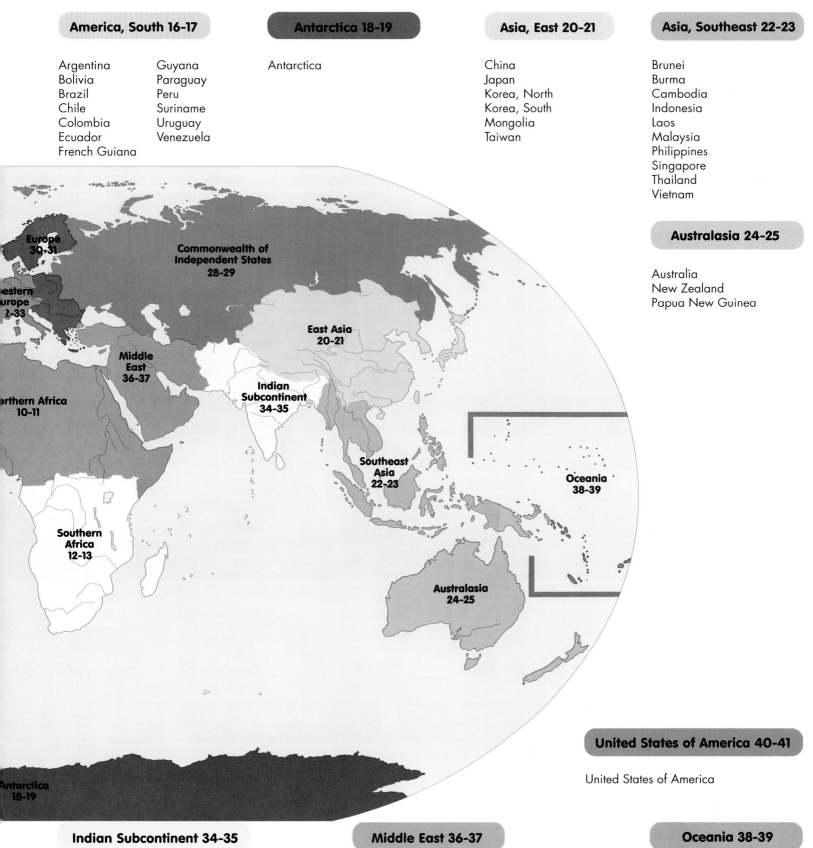

United States of America 40-41

United States of America

Indian Subcontinent 34-35

Afghanistan
Bangladesh
Bhutan
India
Maldives
Nepal
Pakistan
Sri Lanka

Middle East 36-37

Bahrain	Saudi Arabia
Cyprus	Syria
Iran	Turkey
Iraq	United Arab Emirates
Israel	Yemen
Jordan	
Kuwait	
Lebanon	
Oman	
Qatar	

Oceania 38-39

Fiji
Kiribati
Nauru
Solomon Islands
Tonga
Tuvalu
Vanuatu
Western Samoa

Oil has brought considerable wealth to many of the economies in this region, but there are still many countries with a large proportion of their work forces engaged in agriculture, which is constantly threatened by drought.

The Origins and Functions of Money

Before money was invented, a system of exchange took place called "barter" – goods were exchanged directly for other goods. In primitive societies, this still goes on to some extent. A farmer may swap a bag of flour for a pair of shoes, for example. In order to do this, however, the farmer must find someone else who wants the flour and has the shoes in the right size. Barter is therefore time-consuming and requires both parties to want the same deal. Deciding how much each item is worth in relation to another could also create heated arguments. It was not surprising that a better system of exchange was developed long ago.

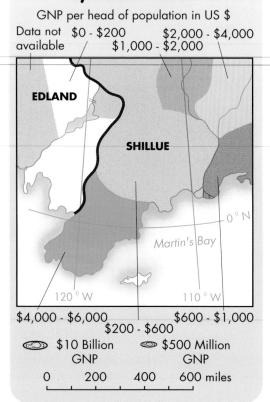

What the colors and symbols mean

GNP per head of population in US $

Data not available	$0 - $200	$2,000 - $4,000
	$1,000 - $2,000	

EDLAND

SHILLUE

0° N

Martin's Bay

120° W   110° W

$4,000 - $6,000 $600 - $1,000
$200 - $600

⬭ $10 Billion GNP   ⬭ $500 Million GNP

0   200   400   600 miles

Bartering

The first traders exchanged or bartered. Flour is bartered for a goat, the goat for rice and grain.

The goat is lastly exchanged for earthenware (pottery). Bartering was not easy as each person had to agree on the value of different goods.

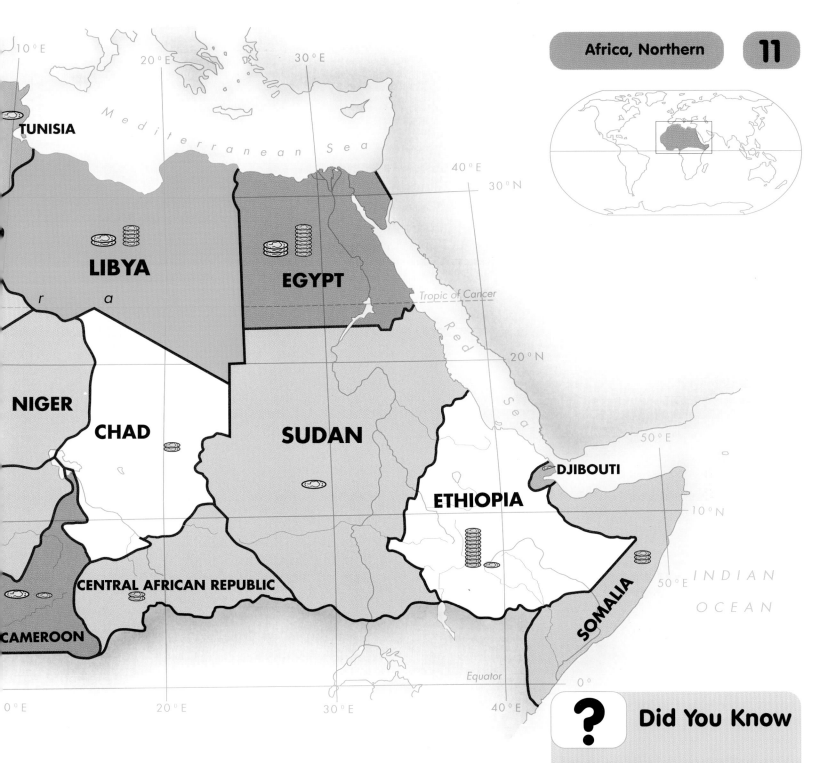

Money can be defined as anything that is generally acceptable as a means of exchanging goods or settling debts. What makes it acceptable will be that it is durable so that it can change hands many times, portable so that it can be carried around, and divisible so that goods can be exchanged in varying quantities. It should also be generally recognizable, and its value should not vary too frequently.

Widely used forms of money in the past have been cows, shells, metals, salt, and stones. Even today, in some rural parts of the less developed world, wealth is measured in cattle.

Currencies

Egypt: Egyptian pound = 100 piastres

Gambia: Dalasi = 100 butut

Mauritania: Ouguiya = 5 khoums

Nigeria: Naira = 100 kobo

Sudan: Sudanese pound = 100 piastres

Tunisia: Tunisian dinar = 1,000 millimes

? Did You Know

★ The Chinese first used cowrie shells as coins. Later they made bronze coins in the shape of cowrie shells.

★ Bartering was first recorded in Egypt over 4,500 years ago.

★ In the past people have used many different things as money. Among them were salt, cocoa beans, grain, cows, sharks' teeth, and precious stones.

★ Aztecs used cocoa beans as money.

Africa, Southern

Mining and agriculture are the main economic activities in southern Africa. Steady growth has been badly hampered by political unrest. South Africa is the most powerful economy, and other nations in this area struggle to free themselves from dependence on this more advanced economy.

Origins of Money

Coins were first made on the coast of Asia Minor in the 8th century. They were made of electrum, or pale gold, a mixture of gold and silver. Croesus, King of Lydia, famous for his great wealth, was the first to introduce gold coins. The right of making coins belonged to the king alone, though governors of provinces were sometimes allowed to strike silver coins.

The early Roman coins were heavy and made of bronze. There are stories of farmers taking their money to market in carts. These were replaced in the 2nd century BC by a silver "denarius," which Julius Caesar, at the height of his reign, had decorated with his head.

The first important European coin was the bezant, which remained the standard gold coin of trade until the florin and ducat were coined in the 13th century. The British gold sovereign and the half sovereign have been of international importance since the 19th century.

Early Anglo-Saxon coins were simple crude imitations, but during the 8th century, King Offa spread the use of the silver penny. These were often cut in half or clipped for convenience in business. From time to time they were melted down and remade.

Making a coin collection

Coin collecting is one of the most popular hobbies in the world and can be a lot of fun. You can begin a coin collection very easily as you do not need expensive equipment. Listed below is all you need to start.

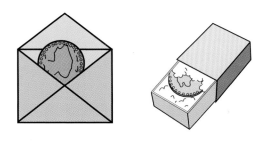

Label the coins and keep them somewhere safe, e.g. paper envelopes or a cardboard box.

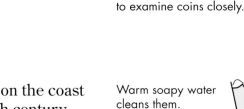

Use a magnifying glass to examine coins closely.

Warm soapy water cleans them.

Use a sharpened matchstick or toothpick to pick off small pieces of dirt.

A soft cloth to dry the coins.

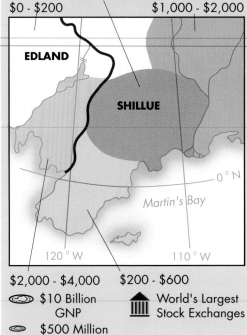

What the colors and symbols mean

GNP per head of population in US $

$0 - $200

$600 - $1,000

$1,000 - $2,000

EDLAND

SHILLUE

$2,000 - $4,000

$200 - $600

$10 Billion GNP

$500 Million GNP

World's Largest Stock Exchanges

120° W   110° W

0° N

Martin's Bay

0   200   400   600 miles

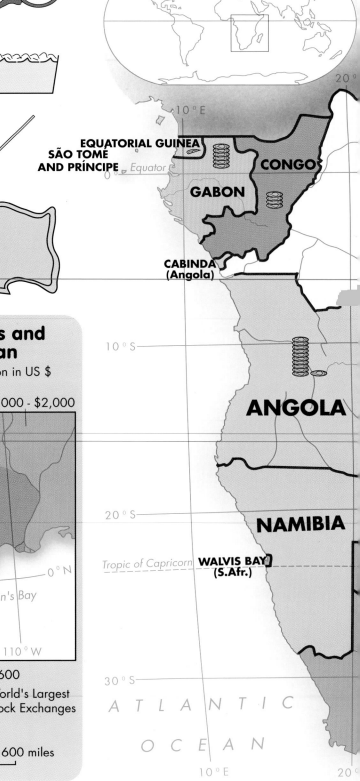

EQUATORIAL GUINEA
SÃO TOMÉ AND PRÍNCIPE *Equator* 0°
GABON
CONGO
CABINDA (Angola)
10° E
20°
10° E
0°
ANGOLA
10° S
NAMIBIA
20° S
Tropic of Capricorn **WALVIS BAY (S.Afr.)**
30° S
A T L A N T I C
O C E A N
10° E
20

Did You Know

★ It is thought that coins were invented by Croesus, King of Lydia. Lydia is now part of modern Turkey. Croesus used nuggets of gold and silver that were hammered into shape and marked to show their value.

★ The world's smallest coin weighed only 0.002 grams and was from Nepal.

Currencies

Angola: Kwanza = 100 lwei

Lesotho: Loti = 100 lisente

Malawi: Kwacha = 100 tambala

Seychelles: Seychelles rupee = 100 cents

South Africa: Rand = 100 cents

Zambia: Kwacha = 100 ngwee

Examples of early coins

Lydian Electrum Coins

Head

A lion's head was the emblem of the king of Lydia

Tail

Early Roman bronze coin

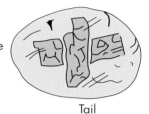

Head

Tail

King Offa's silver penny

Head

Tail

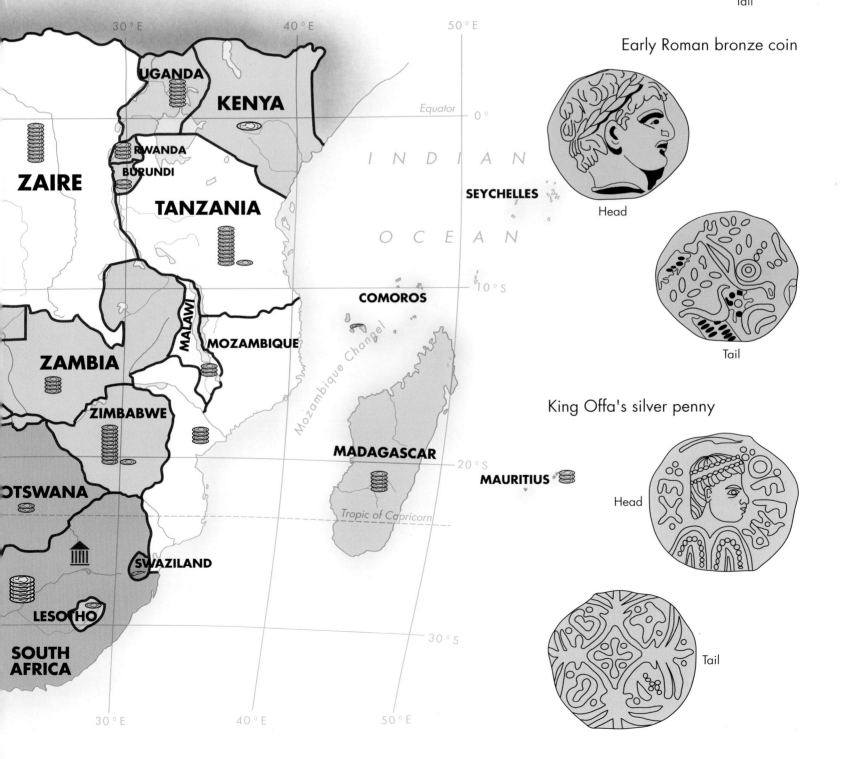

Many of the small nations of Central America have economies linked to just one single export crop, such as sugar, bananas, or coffee. This makes them very vulnerable to price fluctuations. Steady growth has been severely hampered by natural disasters and political unrest.

How Coins Were Made

Early coins were made one at a time by striking a piece of metal between two engraved dies called a pile and a trussel. Because the coins were poorly made, it was easy for dishonest people to clip off parts of the coin, melt all the bits together, and resell them. In order to stop this, designs were made to cover the whole coin.

King Henry VIII of England increased the amount of base metal added to the precious gold and silver in the coin. As the shilling was used, the thin covering of silver plate wore off, leaving copper showing through in the center of the coin, on the nose of the King's face. He became known as Old Coppernose.

"Old Coppernose"

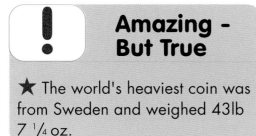
Amazing – But True

★ The world's heaviest coin was from Sweden and weighed 43lb 7 ¼ oz.

Did You Know

★ The writing on coins is often in a kind of code to save space.

★ Coins have a grooved edge because in the past dishonest traders filed down the edges to remove some of the precious metal.

The original design for a coin is drawn by an artist.

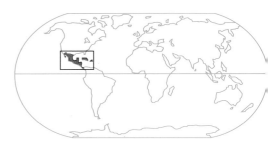

How Coins Are Made

Today all coins are made by machinery in mints. A design is drawn by an artist, and an engraver works on a plaster model, which is then made into a rubber mold. This is then electroplated with nickel and copper. Metals are weighed and carefully checked before the molten metal is poured into a holding furnace, from which it is drawn into a continuous strip. Rolling mills reduce the strip to the exact thickness of the coin that is to be made. Coin-sized disks are then punched from the strip on a blanking press.

The blanks are heated to soften them; then they are brought together with the dies on the coining press. Samples are taken from each batch to check for quality. A machine counts the coins and sews them into bags before passing them to the strongroom to await distribution.

An engineer works on a plaster model of the artist's design.

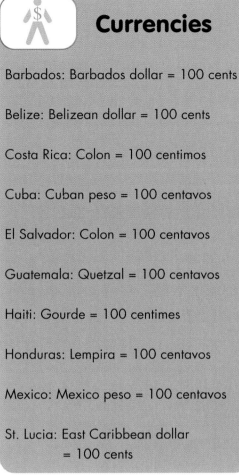

Currencies

Barbados: Barbados dollar = 100 cents

Belize: Belizean dollar = 100 cents

Costa Rica: Colon = 100 centimos

Cuba: Cuban peso = 100 centavos

El Salvador: Colon = 100 centavos

Guatemala: Quetzal = 100 centavos

Haiti: Gourde = 100 centimes

Honduras: Lempira = 100 centavos

Mexico: Mexico peso = 100 centavos

St. Lucia: East Caribbean dollar = 100 cents

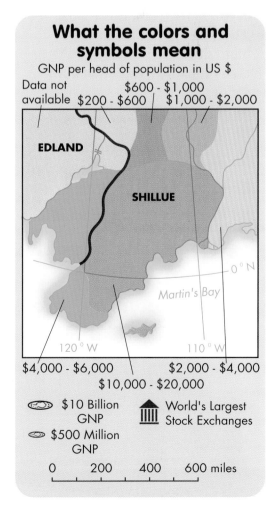

What the colors and symbols mean
GNP per head of population in US $

Data not available — $200 - $600 — $600 - $1,000 — $1,000 - $2,000

$4,000 - $6,000 — $10,000 - $20,000 — $2,000 - $4,000

$10 Billion GNP   World's Largest Stock Exchanges

$500 Million GNP

0   200   400   600 miles

The debt crisis has been the focus of a great deal of concern for the world financial system, as countries in this region, heavily in debt, have no longer been able to repay loans or service their huge interest payments. This has made steady growth very difficult.

Development of Paper Money

The first paper money can be traced back to China during the 7th century. The Italian trader Marco Polo traveled to China and was amazed to see the Chinese use paper money rather than coins. Despite Polo's descriptions, Europeans could not imagine how a piece of paper could be of value. They did not adopt paper money until the 1600s, when banks began to issue paper bills called "bank notes" to despositors and borrowers. These notes could be exchanged for gold and silver coins left in the bank. Until the 1880s, most of the paper notes in circulation were issued by banks or private companies, rather than by governments.

Printing Paper Money

A new banknote is first designed; this is done by an artist and submitted to the secretary of the treasury for approval. Engravers then make a plate of the design. A machine called a transfer press squeezes the design against a soft steel roller, making a raised design on the surface of the roller. The roller is treated with heat to harden it, and another transfer press reproduces the design from the roller 32 times on a printing plate. Each printing plate prints a sheet of 32 bills; another plate is used for the back of the bill.

? Did You Know

★ A banknote is made on special paper; when held up to the light, it reveals a watermark that looks like a picture.

★ A security thread is enclosed in the paper used for currency; this makes copying more difficult for counterfeiters.

Printing paper money

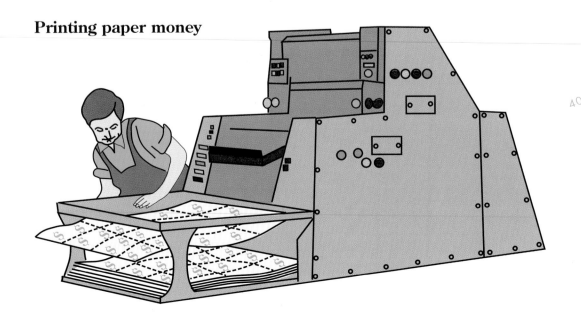

VENEZUELA

GUYANA SURINAME

FRENCH GUIANA

B R A Z I L

B O L I V I A

PARAGUAY

A R G E N T I N A

URUGUAY

Equator 0°

10°N

10°S

20°S

Tropic of Capricorn

30°S

40°S

50°S

40°W

60°W

50°W

70°W

60°W

50°W

40°W

30°S

ATLANTIC

OCEAN

Scotia Sea

Currencies

Argentina: Austral = 100 centavos

Bolivia: Boliviano = 100 centavos

Brazil: New Cruzeiro = 100 centavos

Ecuador: Sucre = 100 centavos

Guyana: Guyana dollar = 100 cents

Paraguay: Guarani = 100 centimos

Peru: Inti = 100 centimos

Suriname: Suriname guilder of Florin = 100 cents

Uruguay: New peso = 100 centesimos

Venezuela: Bolivar = 100 centimos

What the colors and symbols mean

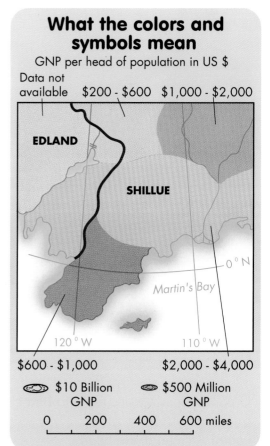

GNP per head of population in US $

Data not available $200 - $600 $1,000 - $2,000

EDLAND

SHILLUE

0°N

Martin's Bay

120°W   110°W

$600 - $1,000 $2,000 - $4,000

$10 Billion GNP $500 Million GNP

0   200   400   600 miles

! Amazing - But True

★ The world's smallest banknote, issued in Morocco, was the size of a postage stamp.

★ The largest banknote was the Chinese 1 kwan printed in the 14th century, measuring 9 x 13 inches.

Because of its harsh climate and terrain, Antarctica has yet to have any significant economic impact on the world. However, it is thought to contain vast mineral resources that might someday prove to be economically viable to extract.

The Chinese used cowrie shells at first as money. Cowrie shells have been used as money in China, India, Thailand, and Africa.

Unusual Forms of Money

In Micronesia stones were used as money. Small stones were exchanged for goods. Large stones like the one below were used to display a person's wealth or to settle disputes. The largest stone money measured 12 feet across.

Colorful beads were used to bater for goods throughout Africa. They were called African trade beads.

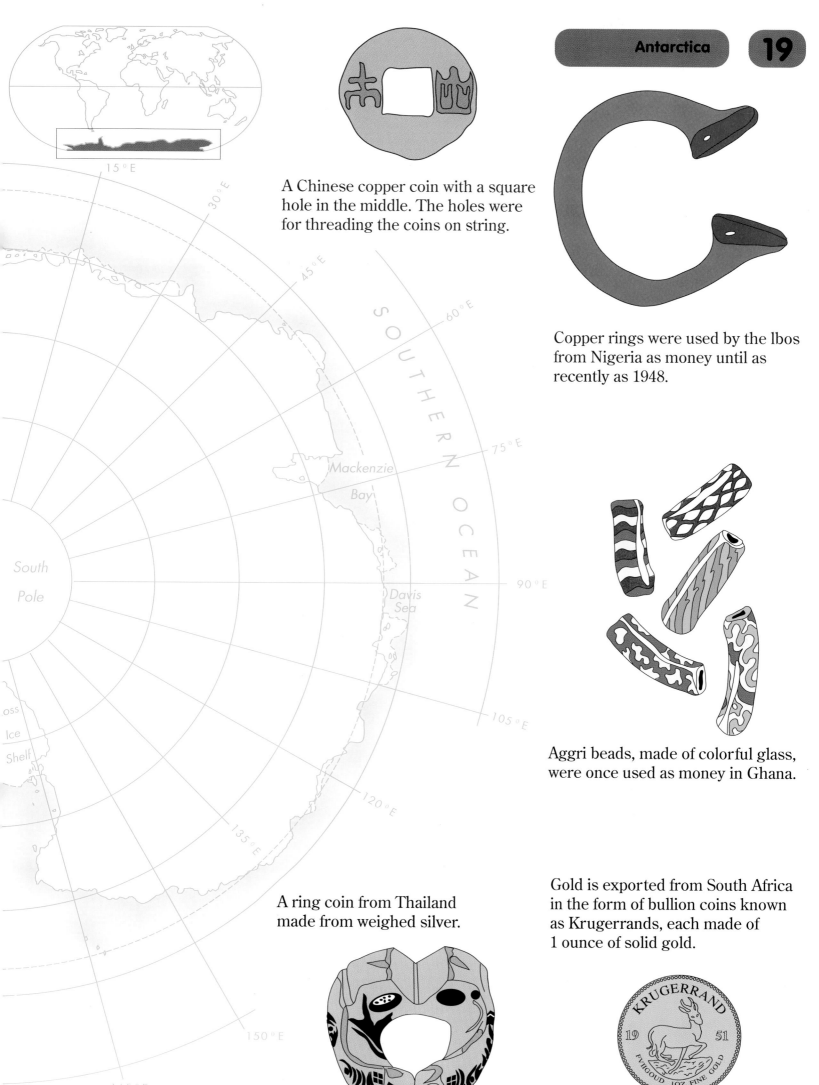

A Chinese copper coin with a square hole in the middle. The holes were for threading the coins on string.

Copper rings were used by the lbos from Nigeria as money until as recently as 1948.

Aggri beads, made of colorful glass, were once used as money in Ghana.

A ring coin from Thailand made from weighed silver.

Gold is exported from South Africa in the form of bullion coins known as Krugerrands, each made of 1 ounce of solid gold.

KRUGERRAND
19 51
FYNGOUD 1OZ FINE GOLD

An abundance of manpower in East Asia has been exploited to good effect in many countries, including Japan, Korea, and Taiwan. Japan has one of the strongest economies in the world.

Economic Systems in the World

A free-market economy (also known as laissez faire) is one in which wants are expressed by individual consumers in the marketplace, and individual producers are free to try and satisfy these wants. The government does not interfere but allows people to produce what they like. If something is difficult to make and raw materials are scarce, its price may be high. If it is easy to make and raw materials are abundant, and it may be cheap. Individuals can compete against each other to produce goods, and this should keep prices at a minimum. The main reason for producing goods is to make a profit.

A command, or planned, economy has a central authority that organizes all the factors of production. China and the former Soviet Union are two examples of this type of economy. The idea behind these economies is to plan everything so there is a more equal distribution of income. In a free-market economy there are winners and losers in business; there are people with inherited wealth and the unemployed. The planned economy tries to iron out these inequalities. The government plans its use of labor and raw materials not to make a profit but to satisfy what they believe to be the "needs" of the consumers. The problems that arise in these economies are mainly involved with the difficulty in planning the use of so many resources.

Mixed economies are the most common today, as no "pure" free-market economies actually exist. Governments play an essential part in the running of their countries and intervene to try and correct some of the unfairness of the free-market economy. They do this by taxing the rich more heavily and redistributing the money to the poor. Through taxation they provide education and health services and may take measures to try to prevent excessive unemployment and inflation, which cause people great hardships.

Countries such as the USA and Britain still let a large part of their economies be determined by the market and individual freedom of choice. In the USA, government activity is kept to a minimum, while in other mixed economies such as those of Scandinavia the government plays a more significant role in the organization of resources.

An economy is made up of services, goods and money. On the left you can see how money goes from the people to industry and back to the people through wages.

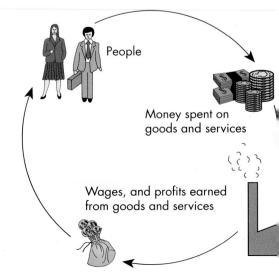

People

Money spent on goods and services

Wages, and profits earned from goods and services

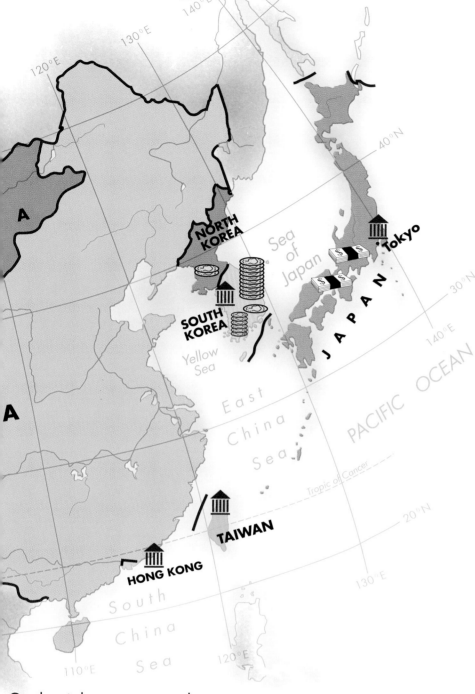

On the right you can see how people provide the skills to produce goods for industry that are then bought by people.

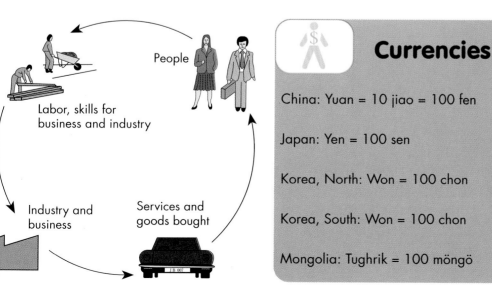

People

Labor, skills for business and industry

Industry and business

Services and goods bought

Currencies

China: Yuan = 10 jiao = 100 fen

Japan: Yen = 100 sen

Korea, North: Won = 100 chon

Korea, South: Won = 100 chon

Mongolia: Tughrik = 100 möngö

Amazing - But True

★ More money is spent on arms in the world than on education, health, or any other form of development.

★ The cost of the 10-year campaign to eradicate smallpox worldwide was less than three hours' spending on arms.

★ The wealth required to provide adequate food, water, education, health, and housing for everyone in the world for a whole year is equivalent to the amount spent on arms every two weeks.

What the colors and symbols mean

GNP per head of population in US $

$600 - $1,000

$200 - $600 $2,000 - $4,000

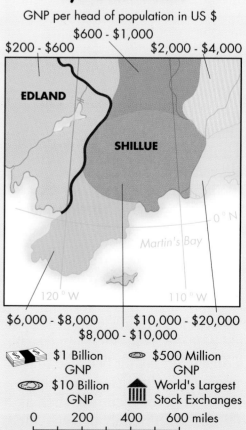

EDLAND

SHILLUE

Martin's Bay

$6,000 - $8,000 $10,000 - $20,000
       $8,000 - $10,000

$1 Billion GNP $500 Million GNP

$10 Billion GNP   World's Largest Stock Exchanges

0   200   400   600 miles

Rice, timber, and rubber were once the mainstays of many of the Southeast Asian economies, but attempts are being made to diversify into manufacturing industries. Thailand is achieving some success at developing textile and clothing industries.

Inflation

Inflation is a continual rise in the general level of prices. If an economy is left alone it will tend to have booms and slumps; this is called the trade cycle. Governments try to keep these fluctuations from becoming too extreme.

Inflation tends to be the result of a booming economy in which too much spending is taking place in relation to the goods being produced. High unemployment is often associated with slumps in the economy. These problems can become really severe if they are not controlled. If the general rise in prices continues extremely quickly and by a great amount, the result may be hyperinflation.

In Germany between 1920 and 1923, inflation reached a staggering 24,000% before the economy and the currency totally collapsed. It had started with a general rise in inflation of 36% in the first year, followed by 63% in the second and 3,300% in the third. In the end, a new currency had to be introduced with one new mark equal to 100,000 million old marks. Money for simple things like a loaf of bread had to be carried in a suitcase.

Hyperinflation causes great instability in a country and prevents people from saving because the value of money falls so quickly. People on fixed incomes, such as retirees, suffer badly because their money buys less.

Currencies

Brunei: Brunei dollar = 100 cents

Burma: Kyat = 100 pyas

Cambodia: New riel = 100 sen

Indonesia: Rupiah = 100 sen

Thailand: Baht = 100 satangs

Vietnam: New dong = 10 xu

! Amazing – But True

★ The world's worst inflation was in Hungary in June 1946, when the 1931 gold pengo was valued at 130 million trillion paper pengos.

% Countries with the highest inflation 1984 – 89

Bookmakers at a race track.

Gambling

Gambling is the act of betting on the outcome of a chance happening, a race, a game, or an event. Gamblers enjoy the challenge and risk of testing their skill in judging an outcome, knowing the rules of an event sufficiently well to understand which bets offer the best value. The usual aim of gambling is to make quick money. However, all gambling by definition is subject to chance, and many see it as a great and destructive evil, ruining lives and causing hardship for gamblers' families.

In many parts of the world, gambling of various sorts is illegal. In other places it is carried out under the watchful eye of the government. Casino gambling, for example, is a very profitable business in some areas, bringing with it a valuable tourist trade. Casino gambling consists of table games of craps and roulette and card games of baccarat and blackjack. Slot machines and poker machines are often found in casinos, and these are responsible for a huge turnover of money.

Gambling on sporting events is a popular form of betting, and one of the most widespread of these is horse racing. At race tracks odds are offered on each horse winning, and the bettors back their skill at judging an outcome at the best price. If the odds are 5 to 1, the bettor would get back $5 on every $1 that was bet. Bookmakers, or bookies, are people who make a business out of offering odds on all sorts of events and paying out money if bettors win.

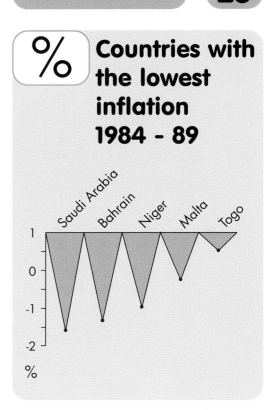

Countries with the lowest inflation 1984 - 89

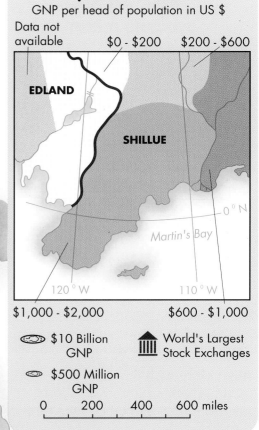

What the colors and symbols mean
GNP per head of population in US $

Data not available

$0 - $200

$200 - $600

EDLAND

SHILLUE

Martin's Bay

120° W   110° W   0° N

$1,000 - $2,000 $600 - $1,000

$10 Billion GNP   World's Largest Stock Exchanges

$500 Million GNP

0   200   400   600 miles

Traditionally dependent on agricultural products, particularly wool, wheat, beef, lamb, and dairy products, Australia and New Zealand have had to look for new markets in order to achieve growth. Closer trading links with Asia have been sought.

Cost of Living

A cost of living index — compiled from a survey of prices for the following items: a shopping basket of food; alcoholic beverages; personal care items; tobacco; utilities; clothing; domestic help; recreation and entertainment — allows a comparison to be made between different countries.
In 1989 the cheapest countries to live in were: Argentina, Brazil, Ecuador, Hungary, India, Nigeria, Paraguay, Venezuela, Yugoslavia, and Zimbabwe. The most expensive were: Cameroon, Congo, Gabon, Iran, Ivory Coast, Japan, Libya, Norway, Taiwan, and Togo.

Consumer Spending

Throughout the world the largest amount of consumer spending is on food (including alcohol and tobacco); however, wealthier countries spend a smaller share of income on food. In industrialized countries an average of 21% of consumer expenditure is on food, while in Africa it is 45%.

Unlike other spending on necessities, the proportion of income devoted to housing tends to rise with income. As income increases in richer countries, owner occupation replaces renting, and family homes replace apartments. In many countries houses are used as a long-term investment and insurance against inflation.

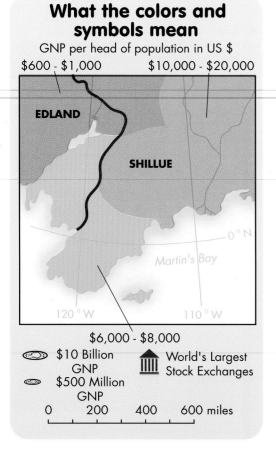

What the colors and symbols mean
GNP per head of population in US $

$600 - $1,000 $10,000 - $20,000

EDLAND

SHILLUE

Martin's Bay

$6,000 - $8,000

$10 Billion GNP

$500 Million GNP

World's Largest Stock Exchanges

0   200   400   600 miles

The holey dollar was the currency of New South Wales, Australia from 1813 until 1822. The middle was also official currency.

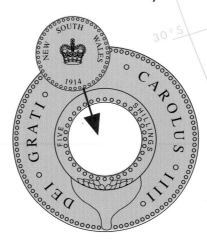

Arafura Sea

INDIAN OCEAN

AUSTR

Tropic of Capricorn

Great Australian Bigh

INDIAN OCEAN

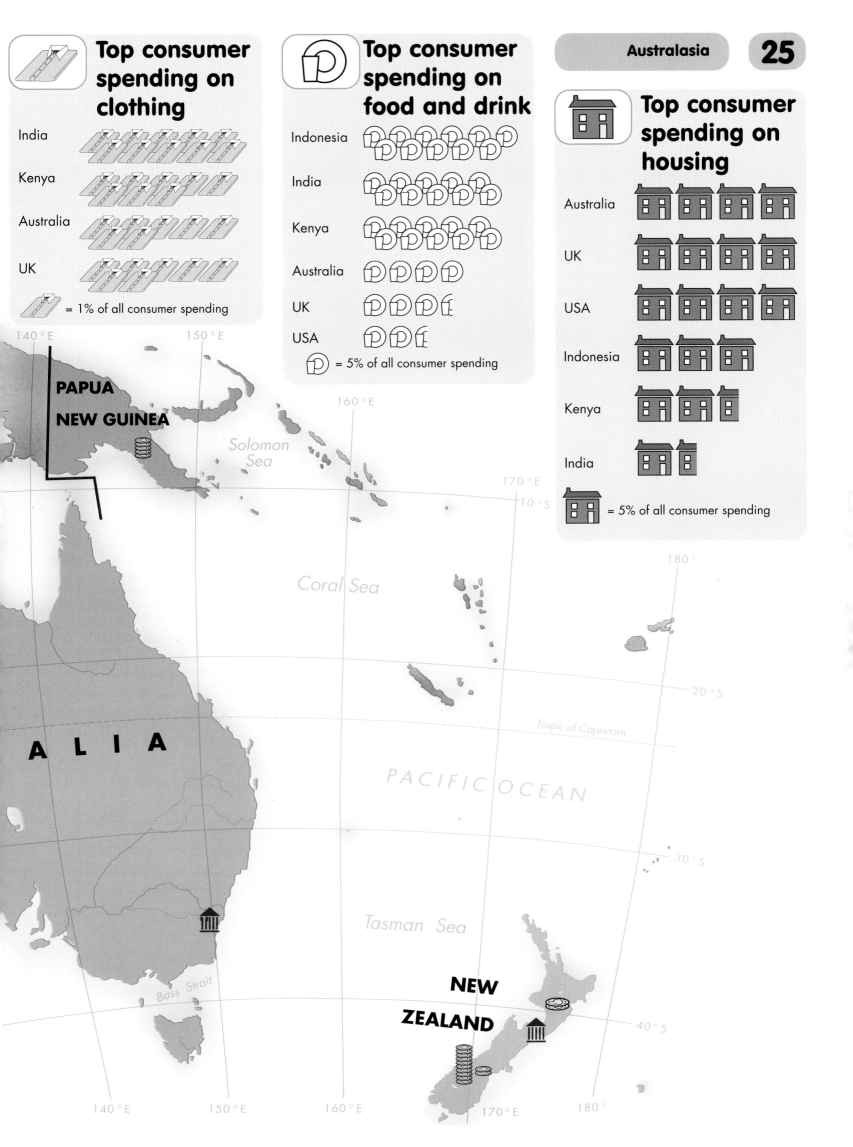

Top consumer spending on clothing

India
Kenya
Australia
UK

= 1% of all consumer spending

Top consumer spending on food and drink

Indonesia
India
Kenya
Australia
UK
USA

= 5% of all consumer spending

Top consumer spending on housing

Australia
UK
USA
Indonesia
Kenya
India

= 5% of all consumer spending

PAPUA NEW GUINEA

Solomon Sea

Coral Sea

PACIFIC OCEAN

Tropic of Capricorn

ALIA

Tasman Sea

NEW ZEALAND

Bass Strait

Rich resources of oil, natural gas, coal and hydroelectricity, along with abundant raw materials of minerals and timber, have given Canada a huge advantage over most industrial economies. Trade is closely linked with the United States.

Economic Strength

The usual way that a country's economic strength is assessed is by its gross domestic — or national — product (GDP or GNP). This is a calculation of the total value of goods and services produced in a given year.

The GDP is the most widely used tool to measure the relative economic strength of different countries.

The top 10 richest countries are mostly developed nations. The size of population ensures that the CIS, China, and India figure high on the list, though in terms of GDP per capita they are relatively poor.

The ten richest countries are: Canada, China, CIS, France, Germany, India, Italy, Japan, UK, and USA.

GDP can be measured in three ways: by adding up the total output of all goods and services in the economy; by measuring expenditure on all goods and services; or by measuring income generated on the production of goods and services. In theory, the answer should be the same for each sum. However, there are problems in getting GDP figures for certain countries. Those devastated by war, such as Kuwait, pose obvious problems, but it is equally difficult to make calculations for planned economies.

Amazing - But True

★ Half the population of the world earns only 5% of the world's total wealth.

★ As a check is only an instruction to a bank, it can be written on anything. In the past people have written checks on such things as stone slabs, bananas, and cows.

What the colors and symbols mean

GNP per head of population in US $

$600 - $1,000

EDLAND

SHILLUE

Martin's Bay

120° W   110° W

Data not available $10,000 - $20,000

$10 Billion GNP   World's Largest Stock Exchanges

$500 Million GNP

0   200   400   600 miles

Plastic Money

Where once people found money a convenient way of buying goods and services, today credit cards or plastic cards are replacing coins and notes. Many transactions now exist only as data on computers.

Credit Cards

There are many different sorts of credit cards that enable a consumer to charge for an item or service at any business place that accepts the card and pay for it later. In order to have a credit card a person must have a record of paying bills on time. The credit card is a small plastic card with the holder's name

Countries with most dollar billionaires

USA	👤 👤 👤 👤 👤 👤 👤 👤 👤 👤 👤 👤 👤
Japan	👤 👤 👤 👤 👤 👤 👤 👤 👤 👤
Germany	👤 👤 👤 👤 👤
Canada	👤 👤

👤 = 5 people worth net $1,000,000,000 or more

and details printed on a magnetic strip. The merchant's computer can read the details on the card and check whether the customer has enough credit to pay for the goods.

When a person buys something with a credit card he or she signs a slip of paper showing how much is owed. The merchant sends this slip to the credit card company, which then settles the bill, deducting a fee for the service. The holder of the card receives a monthly bill that can be paid off in full, or partly paid off. If only part of the bill is paid, interest is charged on the remaining amount.

One example of plastic money

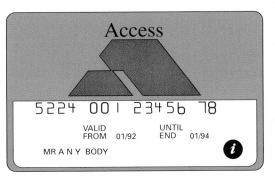

Access

5224 001 23456 78

VALID FROM 01/92   UNTIL END 01/94

MR A N Y BODY

Currencies

Canada: Canadian dollar = 100 cents

Store Cards

These are issued by some big stores so that customers do not need to use other credit cards when making purchases in the store. This solves the problem of having to carry around large sums of money when making purchases.

Despite a wealth of natural resources, economic growth has been painfully slow in the last 10 years. Industry is in need of modernization, transport is poor, and manufactured goods are not on the whole competitive on world markets.

Soviet Economy

The economy was planned, with the government owning most of the nation's land, factories, mines, communication systems, banks, etc. The government had the task of planning and controlling what was produced, how much of it was produced, at what price it was sold, how much those who produce it were paid, and how it was distributed. This was carried out in carefully worked out five-year plans. The first five-year plan, started in 1928, emphasized the production of heavy industrial goods such as chemicals, machine tools, construction materials, and steel.

What the colors and symbols mean

GNP per head of population in US $

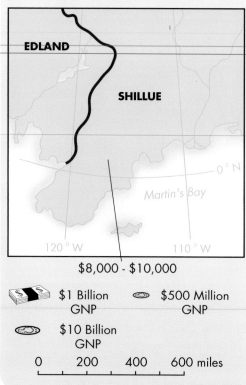

$8,000 - $10,000

📑 $1 Billion GNP   💿 $500 Million GNP

💿 $10 Billion GNP

0   200   400   600 miles

At first the Soviet economy expanded rapidly, but improvement in living standards were slow and tended to lag behind standards in other parts of the world such as the United States.

In particular, the economy suffered from low productivity and a poorly motivated work force. To boost the economy and increase efficiency and try to satisfy consumer demands, a major reform was introduced in the 1980s called "perestroika." This aimed to increase private enterprise and make the economy more competitive in international trade. However, the economy still remains in a desperate state. Bureaucrats, not wishing to be deprived of their power as the country moved toward a market economy, blocked many reforms. Workers were suspicious of new directions and often ignored them; shortages were made even worse by farmers withholding many products from the market.

OF INDEPENDENT STATES

A line of customers waiting outside
a bakery in Moscow.
People sometimes have to wait
many hours to be served.

? **Did You Know**

★ Food shortages in the CIS,
including those of bread and
other basic goods, increased so
much that by 1991 food
rationing was necessary, making
lines for food an everyday
occurrence.

Moscow Bakery

Currencies

CIS: Rubl = 100 Kopeks

Industry has traditionally been very strong in Europe, but there has been a decline in many of the heavy manufacturing industries such as steel, coal and textiles, combined with a rapid expansion in service industries. Inflation, recession, and unemployment are constant threats.

The Development of Banks

Banking began with goldsmiths, many of whom were once located in Lombardy, Italy. They safeguarded gold deposited by customers and acted as pawnbrokers and moneylenders. They carried out their business on wooden benches, and in that way *banco,* the Italian word for "bench," became *bank* in English. The word *bankrupt* also derives from the Italian for "broken bench" — *banca rotta.*
Goldsmiths came to realize that the gold deposits could be loaned out at interest. A receipt was given by the goldsmiths, in the knowledge that it could be used to redeem the gold supply at any time. This was the origin of the banknote. Banks also authorized orders written and signed by depositors for amounts of money to be paid to another person; this was the first version of a modern-day check. Checks became widely used in the 19th century, when printed checks were first issued.
Today banking is an international business. The main functions of banks are to distribute legal tender (money) on behalf of a nation's treasury and to make sure enough cash is available at all times. Banks accept deposits of money.
This money is lent out, and by charging a higher rate of interest to borrowers than they give to depositors, banks make a profit. Banks also collect and transfer money via the check-clearing system, which is the primary type of transaction in industrialized nations.

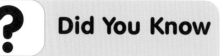

Did You Know

★ Many countries have a central bank to keep watch on private banks.

★ The central bank in Germany is the Deutsche Bundesbank. The central bank in the United Kingdom is the Bank of England. The central bank in the United States is the Federal Reserve System.

★ The Banc' Éireann is a bank on wheels providing a service for far-flung customers in rural southern Ireland.

★ Most of the earliest banks were started by goldsmiths, who had safes for their gold. People then paid to keep their own valuables in the goldsmiths' safes.

How a bank works

Once your money has been deposited into a bank, it is carefully watched and kept safe until you withdraw it in the form of cash, check, or by using a credit card.

Cash

Credit card

Check

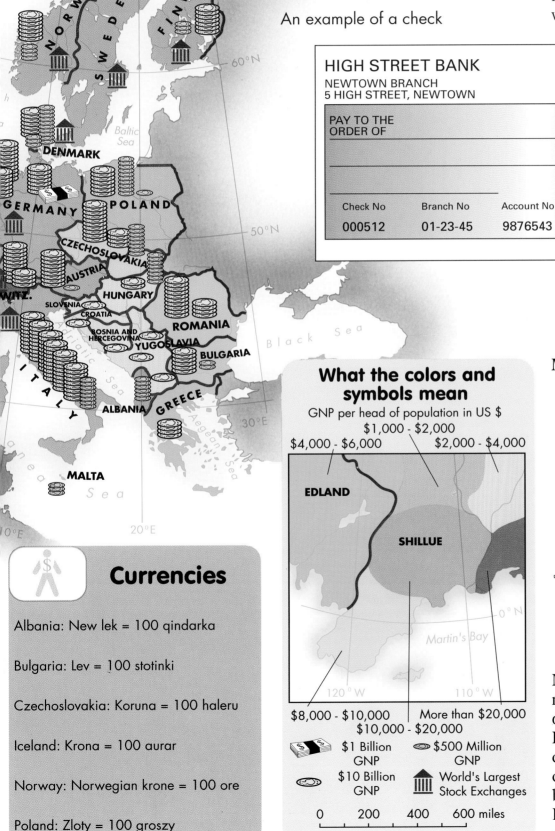

Checks and Bank Cards

A person who has a bank account can instruct the bank to pay for a purchase by writing a check for the amount owing. Checks are specially printed by the bank and are useful because they mean that people do not have to carry around cash. They are also convenient for sending money by mail.

An example of a check

HIGH STREET BANK		19
NEWTOWN BRANCH 5 HIGH STREET, NEWTOWN		01-23-45

PAY TO THE ORDER OF _____ $ _____

Dollars

Check No	Branch No	Account No	
000512	01-23-45	9876543	MR A N Y BODY

Automatic Teller

Bank cards are also used for drawing money in the form of cash from bank dispensing machines. These machines are useful because they enable money to be taken out at any time of the night or day and avoid ther necessity of waiting in line at bank counters for withdrawals.

Maundy Money

Maundy money is specially minted money that the British sovereign distributes in Westminster Abbey, London in a traditional almsgiving ceremony. The ceremony commemorates the Thursday before Good Friday, when at the Last Supper Christ washed the feet of the disciples.

Currencies

Albania: New lek = 100 qindarka

Bulgaria: Lev = 100 stotinki

Czechoslovakia: Koruna = 100 haleru

Iceland: Krona = 100 aurar

Norway: Norwegian krone = 100 ore

Poland: Zloty = 100 groszy

What the colors and symbols mean

GNP per head of population in US $

$1,000 - $2,000

$4,000 - $6,000 $2,000 - $4,000

EDLAND

SHILLUE

Martin's Bay

$8,000 - $10,000   More than $20,000
$10,000 - $20,000

$1 Billion GNP $500 Million GNP

$10 Billion GNP   World's Largest Stock Exchanges

0   200   400   600 miles

Germany is emerging as the economic giant of Europe, but merging the two economies of the East and the West has slowed their progress down in the short term.

The Stock Exchange

A stock exchange is a market where stocks and shares are bought and sold. A stock is a loan to a company or government, and a share gives the lender entitlement to ownership in that company. Prices of stocks and shares move up and down according to demand and supply. Falling profits and strikes could lead to a fall in the share prices of a company, while the rumor of, for instance, a big oil find by a petroleum company might lead to an increase in its share prices. In this way the stock exchange provides accurate market prices. The stock exchange also acts as a kind of barometer of economic performance, since changes in the profitability of industry will be reflected in share price movements. At times stock markets can be very volatile — loss of confidence can lead to panic selling. On October 29, 1929, the New York Stock Exchange registered an exchange of 16,410,030 shares. This was the famous Black Tuesday "crash." The total amount of money lost during the Great Depression between September 1929 and June 1932 was $74 billion.

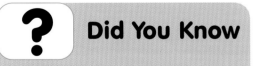

? Did You Know

★ There are 138 stock exchanges in the world.

★ The first European stock exchange was established in Antwerp, Belgium, in 1531.

Different stock markets work at different times

During the busiest time in London's stock exchange they are reacting to the news from the Tokyo stock exchange where work has finished for the day.

In New York work has not yet started. It is only later in the afternoon that London can begin to watch the events on Wall Street, New York.

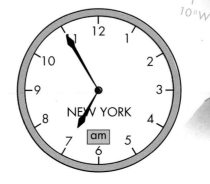

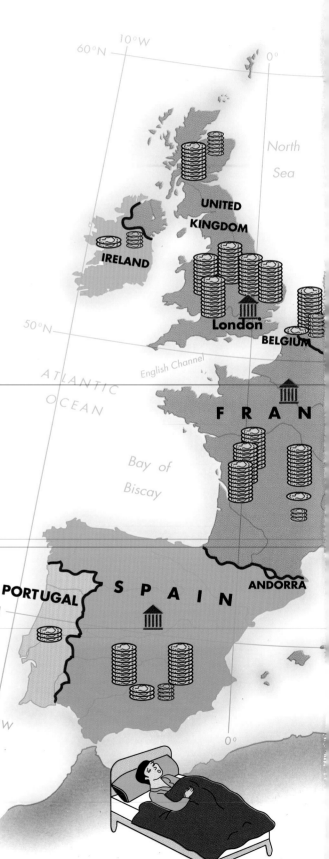

Amazing - But True

★ The stock markets in the US and Japan accounted for more than half the world's capitalization in the early 1990s.

★ Britain's rarest coin is the 1952 George VI half-crown.

What the colors and symbols mean

GNP per head of population in US $

$4,000 - $6,000 $2,000 - $4,000

EDLAND

SHILLUE

Martin's Bay

More than $20,000 $10,000 - $20,000

$1 Billion GNP $500 Million GNP

$10 Billion GNP   World's Largest Stock Exchanges

0   200   400 miles

Currencies

Austria: Schilling = 100 groschen

Finland: = Finland markka = 100 penniä

France: French franc = 100 centimes

Italy: Lira = 100 centesimi

Portugal: Escudo = 100 centavos

Spain: Spanish peseta =1,000 céntimos

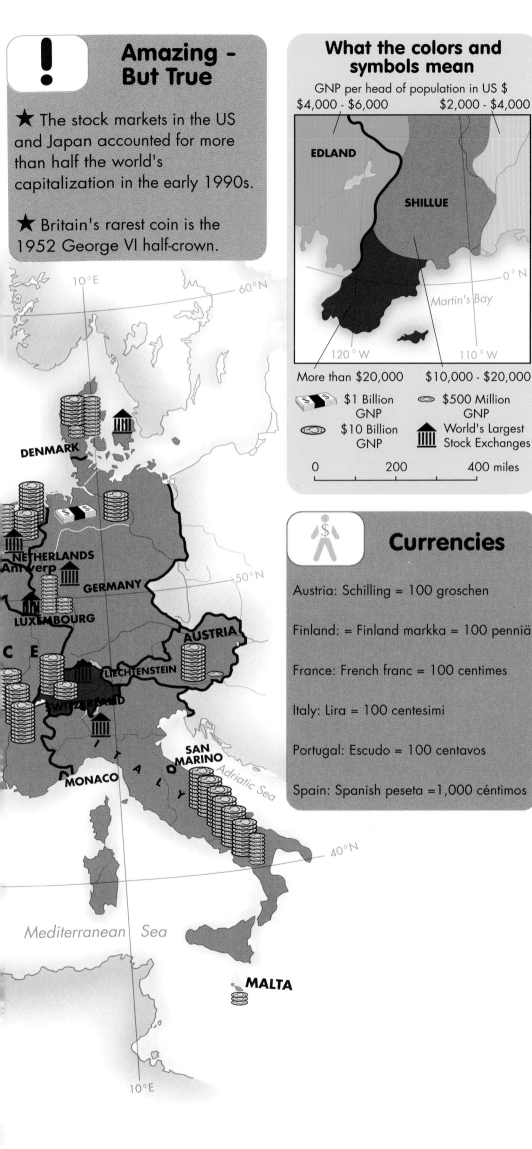

European Community

The European Community is made up of twelve nations: Belgium, Britain, Denmark, France, Greece, Germany, Ireland, Italy, Luxembourg, the Netherlands, Portugal, and Spain.

The EC was originally the idea of a Frenchman, Jean Monnet, who wanted to transform Europe into a kind of United States of Europe, a federation of states working together for political integration. Economic integration is seen as an important step toward this goal. However, progress has been slow. Countries have been reluctant to give up their own sovereignty to EC bureaucracies.

In the 1980s a plan for creating one internal market in Europe by 1992 was created. A large number of changes were to be made, including the removal of all physical barriers including frontier controls; the removal of technical barriers, to be achieved by the adoption of European standards for manufacturing and the removal of national standards; and the removal of tax barriers.

As the deadline for economic unity approaches, however, many countries are getting cold feet. There are grave doubts about the establishment of a single European currency, the Ecu; there is distrust of European bureaucracy, and deepening recession in many European countries has caused governments to rethink many of the EC policies.

The "green revolution" has made India self-sufficient in agriculture; although most people still work on the land, manufacturing industries are expanding rapidly in India and Pakistan. Bangladesh remains one of the poorest and most overcrowded regions of the world.

Foreign Investment

Business and industry need money, but money is largely attracted to areas where it will make the most profit. Most foreign investment flows between the major industrialized nations. About two-thirds of US direct investment abroad is in Canada and the European Economic Community (EEC). Private investment flows from the EEC countries to the USA and other European countries. The ability to attract foreign investment depends on such things as the political stability of a country and its government policy as well as its economic performance.

For "poor" countries that desperately need foreign investment for economic development, the competition for money is difficult. The world recession of the 1980s and the increase in interest rates has meant that many countries could not afford to pay the interest on their foreign loans, let alone pay back the original sums. These countries have to export goods to earn money to pay their foreign debts.

The World Bank acts as a bridge between the rich and poor countries, directing capital from the industrialized nations to the developing world.

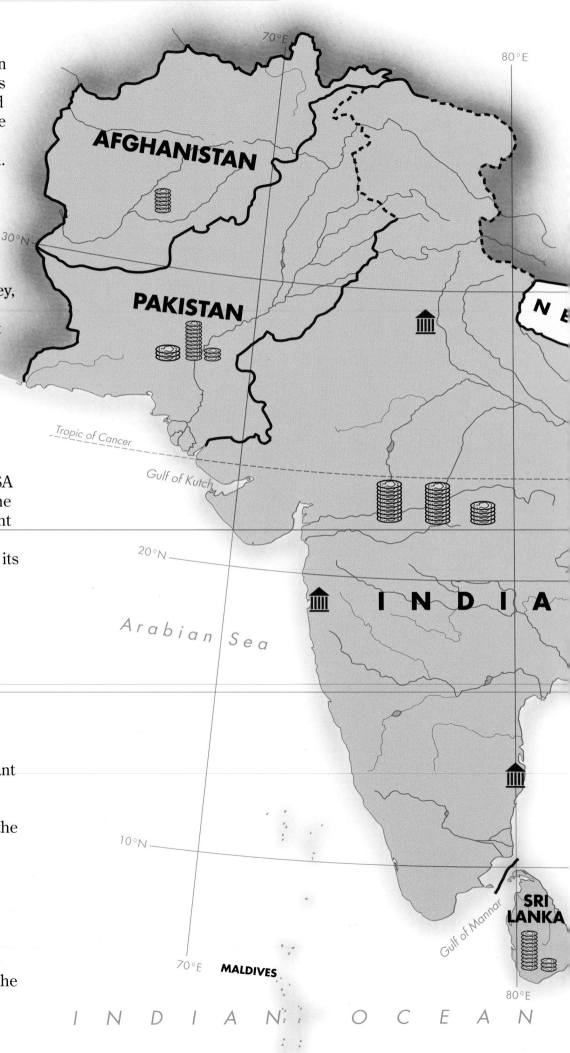

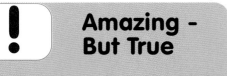

Amazing – But True

★ The largest check ever written was from the American ambassador to the Indian government for $1,279,187,490.

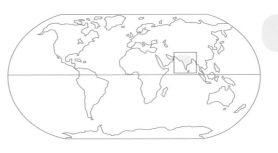

Currencies

Afghanistan: Afghani = 100 puls

Bangladesh: Taka = 100 poisha

Bhutan: Ngultrum = 100 chetrum

India: Rupee = 100 paise

Maldives: Rufiyaa = 100 laaris

Nepal: Nepalese rupee = 100 paisa

Pakistan: Pakistani rupee = 100 paisa

Sri Lanka: Sri Lanka rupee = 100 cents

30°N
90°E
BHUTAN
BANGLADESH
Tropic of Cancer
20°N
Bay of Bengal
90°E
Andaman Sea

International Reserves

International reserves are the country's official holdings of foreign currency, which it uses to stabilize exchange rates and pay international debts. Many countries hold their international reserves in the form of US dollars.

The International Monetary Fund (IMF) is the main organization that aims to improve financial dealings between countries. Members who run into balance of payment difficulties may borrow from the fund.

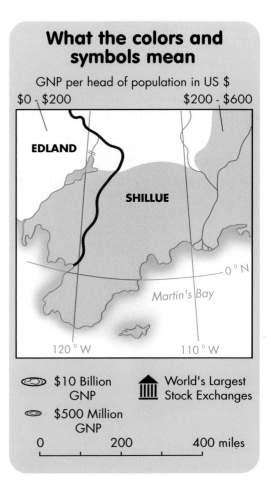

What the colors and symbols mean

GNP per head of population in US $

$0 - $200 $200 - $600

EDLAND

SHILLUE

0°N

Martin's Bay

120°W   110°W

$10 Billion GNP   World's Largest Stock Exchanges

$500 Million GNP

0   200   400 miles

Oil dominates the economies of the Middle East and the wealth generated by this resource has been used to diversify the economies into other industries and to develop agriculture. War has devastated parts of the region in recent years.

Forgery

The crime of forgery has always been considered a serious one, but there have been many examples of people who have tried to profit by producing coins or notes that are imitations.

When money was in the form of gold and silver coins, traders used to try and check that coins were made of the full weight of the metal. Coin balances and weights were one way of checking that the right amount of gold was in a coin. The saying "up to scratch" comes from the old method of using a touchstone and needles. In order to establish the quality of the gold in a coin, a merchant would mark a touchstone with the correct gold carat touch needle and then compare the mark with that left by the coin.

A trader weighing coins to check that they are the full weight of metal.

Governments take great care to ensure that paper money and coins cannot be forged. Banknotes have seals and serial numbers so that they can be traced, and a number of measures to prevent forgeries are used, including exceptionally fine printing techniques, watermarking paper, and inserting strips of metal in the paper.

Black Sea

Aegean Sea

40°N

30°E

40°E

TURKEY

CYPRUS

Mediterranean Sea

LEBANON

SYRIA

IRAQ

ISRAEL **JORDAN**

30°N

30°E

KUWAIT

S A U D I

Tropic of Cancer

A R A B I A

20°N

40°E

YEMEN

Gulf

Did You Know

★ The people with the highest income in the world are the oil rich rulers in the Middle East who receive royalties from each barrel of oil they sell.

Balance of Payments

The difference between a country's receipts of foreign currency and its expenditure of foreign currency is known as its balance of payments. The balance of payments for a country has an effect on the exchange rate. If a country has a balance of payments deficit, more money is flowing out of the country than is coming in; while a balance of payments surplus means that income is greater than expenditure.

Currencies

Iran: Rial = 100 dinars

Iraq: Iraqi dinar = 20 dirhams
= 1,000 fils

Israel: Shekel = 100 agorot

Jordan: Jordanian dinar = 1,000 fils

Kuwait: Kuwaiti dinar = 1,000 fils

Lebanon: Lebanese pound = 100 piastres

Oman: Rial = 1,000 biazas

Qatar: Riyal = 100 dirhams

Saudi Arabia: Saudi Riyal = 100 halalah

Syria: Syrian pound = 100 piastres

Turkey: Turkish lira = 100 kurus

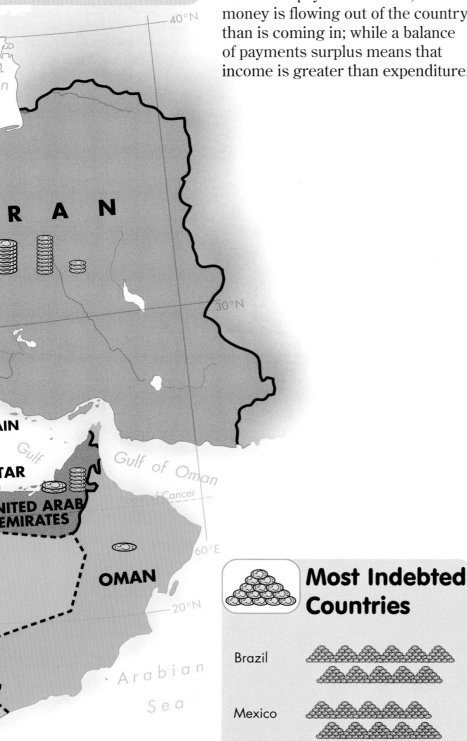

Most Indebted Countries

Brazil

Mexico

Argentina

Poland

Venezuela

= $10,000,000,000

What the colors and symbols mean

GNP per head of population in US $

$1,000 - $2,000

$200 - $600

$2,000 - $4,000

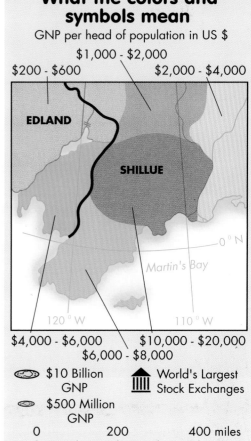

EDLAND

SHILLUE

Martin's Bay

$4,000 - $6,000 $10,000 - $20,000
$6,000 - $8,000

$10 Billion GNP

World's Largest Stock Exchanges

$500 Million GNP

0   200   400 miles

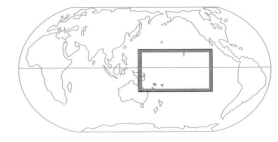

Economically fragile and dependent on outside help, many of the islands of Oceania have just one product that sustains their economy, such as nickel in New Caledonia and phosphates in the Christmas Islands.

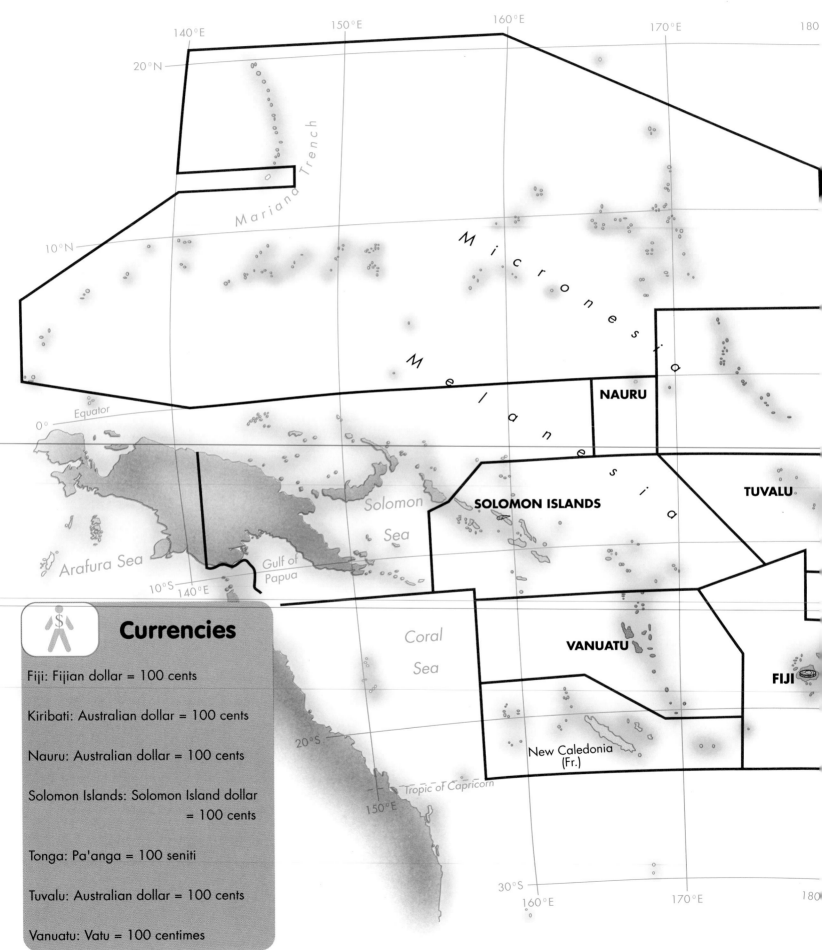

Currencies

Fiji: Fijian dollar = 100 cents

Kiribati: Australian dollar = 100 cents

Nauru: Australian dollar = 100 cents

Solomon Islands: Solomon Island dollar
= 100 cents

Tonga: Pa'anga = 100 seniti

Tuvalu: Australian dollar = 100 cents

Vanuatu: Vatu = 100 centimes

20°N

10°N

Mariana Trench

Micronesia

Melanesia

Equator
0°

NAURU

SOLOMON ISLANDS

TUVALU

Solomon
Sea

Arafura Sea

Gulf of
Papua

10°S
140°E

Coral

Sea

VANUATU

FIJI

New Caledonia
(Fr.)

20°S

Tropic of Capricorn

150°E

30°S
160°E

170°E

180

140°E

150°E

160°E

170°E

180

What the colors and symbols mean

GNP per head of population in US $

Data not available $600 - $1,000

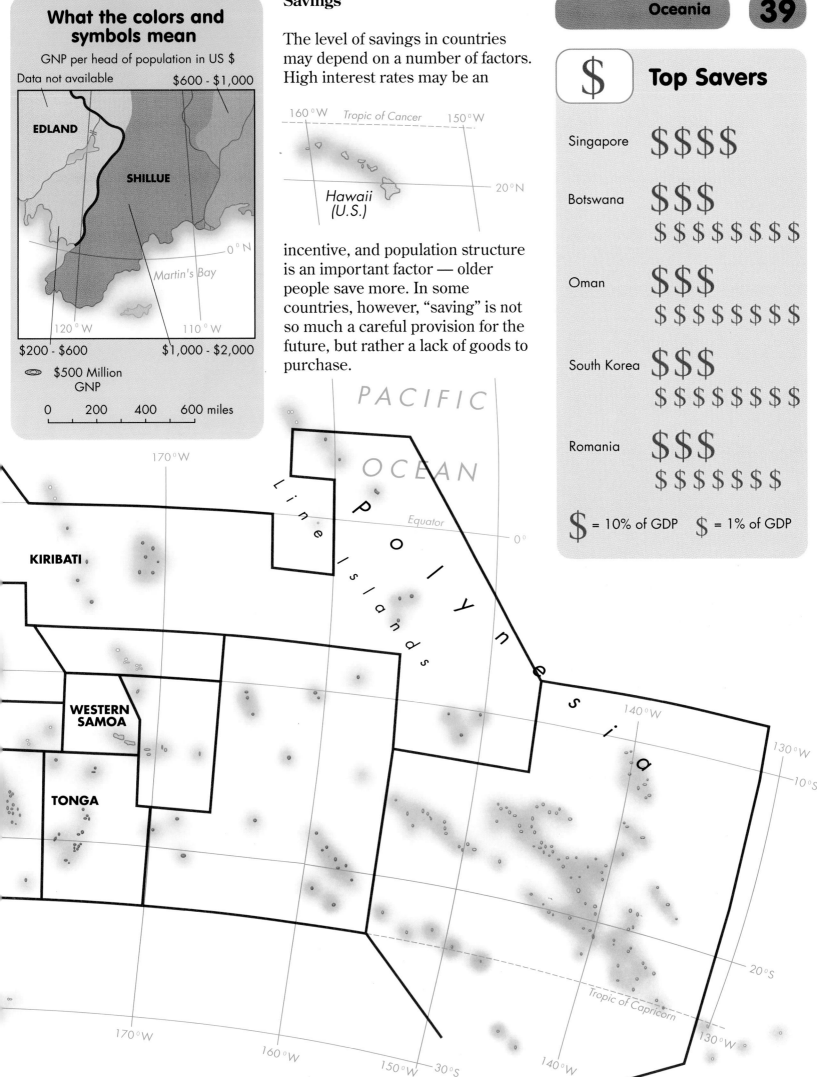

EDLAND

SHILLUE

Martin's Bay

$200 - $600 $1,000 - $2,000

$500 Million
GNP

0   200   400   600 miles

Savings

The level of savings in countries may depend on a number of factors. High interest rates may be an

160°W Tropic of Cancer 150°W

Hawaii
(U.S.)

20°N

incentive, and population structure is an important factor — older people save more. In some countries, however, "saving" is not so much a careful provision for the future, but rather a lack of goods to purchase.

$ **Top Savers**

Singapore $$$

Botswana $$$
$$$$$$$

Oman $$$
$$$$$$$

South Korea $$$
$$$$$$$

Romania $$$
$$$$$$$

$ = 10% of GDP $ = 1% of GDP

PACIFIC

OCEAN

Line Islands

Equator

0°

KIRIBATI

P o l y n e s i a

WESTERN
SAMOA

TONGA

Tropic of Capricorn

170°W
170°W   160°W   150°W   140°W   130°W

30°S

140°W   130°W

10°S

20°S

Excelling in the highly technical industries such as computers, aerospace, and pharmaceuticals, the United States has one of the most diversified and soundest economies in the world. Low tax rates reflect the entrepreneurial ideal at the heart of the economy.

Taxation

The main taxes can be divided into those paid on income and capital, called "direct" taxes, and those paid when money is spent, called "indirect" taxes. Income tax, in effect, redistributes wealth from the rich toward the poor (via social programs). It is a fairly simple tax to collect, as many employers pay the tax directly for their employees, deducting it from the salary before it is paid. However, it is generally a progressive tax; more is paid as income rises. This may become a drawback if there is no incentive to work harder because people may feel that they earn relatively less and pay more tax.

Indirect taxes are paid on goods and services. The taxes are paid by the shops or manufacturers but then passed on to the consumers in the form of higher prices. In the UK, for example, the value added tax or VAT is the most important indirect tax. The advantage of this tax is that it is directly in line with inflation. If prices rise, so does the tax. However, the burden of this tax falls more heavily on the less well off.

Countries vary in the balance of their taxation: some rely more on income taxes, while other gain a larger proportion from indirection taxation. However, a balance is generally thought to be the fairest system.

The government of a country needs to raise taxes in order to provide goods and services that will be shared by consumers. Defense spending is one of the main items in this category. Governments maintain armed forces and spend money on such costly items as aircraft carriers and tanks. Law enforcement is another priority for the government. In addition, other services such as health and education would only be affordable to the rich if the government did not provide them.

Another part of government spending is allocated to caring for those who do not have an income. The very poor, the unemployed, and dependent children are provided for out of taxation.

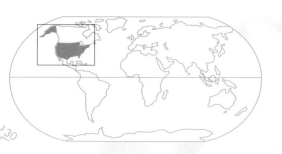

In the United States the Federal Reserve issues paper money called Federal Reserve notes. These have the nation's motto "In God We Trust."

An example of a Federal Reserve note.

? Did You Know

★ The countries with the lowest tax in the world are Bahrain, Brunei, Kuwait, and Qatar (where there is no tax at all).

★ The highest taxation rate is in Norway. Some people pay more than 100% of their taxable income.

★ The highest recorded personal tax demand is one for $336 million on the estate of Howard Hughes.

Average Annual Salary of Some Jobs in the USA

Lawyer	$96,720
Airline Pilot	$85,592
Aerospace Engineer	$85,280
Doctor	$84,760
Financial Manager	$81,952
Chemical Engineer	$81,640
Personnel Manager	$81,640
Securities & Financial Services Salesman	$79,872
Education Administrator	$78,728
College Professor	$78,208

New York

STATES

AMERICA

ATLANTIC OCEAN

Gulf of Mexico

Tropic of Cancer

What the colors and symbols mean

GNP per head of population in US $

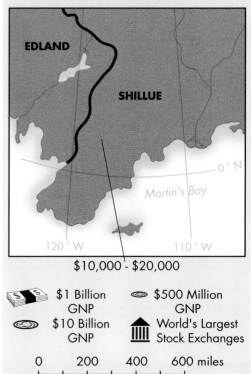

EDLAND

SHILLUE

Martin's Bay

$10,000 - $20,000

$1 Billion GNP	$500 Million GNP
$10 Billion GNP	World's Largest Stock Exchanges

0   200   400   600 miles

Balance of Payments
The record of a country's international transactions over a given time. These are in the form of imports and exports of goods (visible trade) and services (invisible trade).

Bureaucracy
A system of administration based on organization into many offices, involving a division of labor into many layers of responsibility. It has come to have the meaning of unnecessary official procedures.

Capital
Wealth that is capable of generating income or of being used to make further wealth. Capitalism is a system in which work is undertaken for individual reward, where workers are free to make their own contracts, and capital goods can be owned by individuals.

Consumers
Persons who buy goods and services for their own needs.

Cost of Living
A measure of the income required to purchase essential goods. Usually the cost of living index (also known as the Consumer Index) is based on a standard "basket" of goods.

Counterfeiting
The illegal production of false money for gain. Counterfeiting is a form of forgery, using money as the means of fraud.

Entrepreneur
A person in a capitalist economy who is willing to risk capital to start a commercial venture.

Exchange Rate
The value of one country's currency in terms of another. International trade and tourism make it very important that exchange rates remain fairly stable rather than going up and down in an unpredictable manner.

Floating Exchange Rate
Exchange rates that are not fixed but are able to go up and down according to supply and demand.

Fluctuation
The act of shifting back and forth uncertainly.

Incentive
A motivating influence or a stimulus. In business an incentive may be an additional amount paid or a reward for working harder.

Indirect Taxation
Taxes on goods and services that are collected through traders and manufacturers.

Inflation
A fall in the actual value of money. Inflation may be a result of an increase in the supply of money, high government spending, the creation of credit (for example, through credit cards), or high wage settlements.

Interest
The price paid for the use of money. If credit is given or a loan is taken interest is the cost of that service.

Legal Tender
Money or currency in the form of notes and coins that must by law be accepted in payment of a debt.

Nonlegal Tender
Checks, credit cards, and other means of settling debts that do not have to be accepted by law.

Pawnbroker
A dealer who is licensed to lend money at a certain rate of interest in exchange for personal possessions. If the loan is not repaid within a specified time the possessions can be sold.

Recession
A decline in the economy in which demand falls, investment slows down, and business failures become more common.

Treasury
The government department in charge of finance.

Volatile
Capable of sudden change.

Boulding, Kenneth E. *The World as a Total System.*
Beverly Hills, CA: Sage Publications, 1985.

Blaug, Mark. *The Methodology of Economics, or How Economists Explain.*
New York: Cambridge University Press, 1980.

Bruntland, G. H. *Our Common Economic Future: World Commission on Environment and Development.*
New York: Oxford University Press, 1987.

Canavan, Bernard. *Economics for Beginners.*
New York: Pantheon, 1983.

Cole, George Douglas Howard. *Studies in World Economics.*
Freeport, NY: Books for Libraries Press, 1967.

Gailbraith, John Kenneth. *Economics in Perspective: A Critical History.*
New York: Houghton Mifflin, 1988.

Goldberg, Jake. *Economics and the Environment.*
New York: Chelsea House, 1993.

Hamrin, R. D. *America's New Economy: A Basic Guide.*
New York: Watts, 1988.

Kolko, Joyce. *Restructuring the World Economy.*
New York: Pantheon, 1988.

Lee, Susan. *Susan Lee's ABZs of Economics.*
New York: Simon & Schuster, 1988.

This index is designed to help you to find places shown on the maps. The index is in alphabetical order and lists all towns, countries, and physical features. After each entry extra information is given to describe the entry and to tell you which country or continent it is in.

The next column contains the latitude and longitude figures. These are used to help locate places on maps. They are measured in degrees. The blue lines drawn across the map are lines of latitude. The equator is at latitude 0°. All lines above the equator are referred to as °N (north of the equator). All lines below the equator are referred to as °S (south of the equator).

The blue lines drawn from the top to the bottom of the map are lines of longitude. The 0° line passes through Greenwich, London, and is known as the Greenwich Meridian. All lines of longitude join the North Pole to the South Pole. All lines to the right of the Greenwich Meridian are referred to as °E (east of Greenwich), and all lines to the left of the Greenwich Meridian are referred to as °W (west of Greenwich).

The final column indicates the number of the page where you will find the place for which you are searching.

If you want to find out where the Gulf of Thailand is, look it up in the alphabetical index. The entry will read:

Name, Description	Location		Page
	Lat.	Long.	
Thailand, Gulf of, Asia	11°N	101°E	22

Turn to page 22 in your atlas. The Gulf of Thailand is located where latitude 11°N meets longitude 101°E. Place a pencil along latitude 11°N. Now take another pencil and place it along 101°E. Where the two pencils meet is the location of the Gulf of Thailand. Practice finding places in the index and on the maps.

Name, Description	Location		Page
	Lat.	Long.	
A			
Aden, Gulf of, Middle East	12°N	47°E	36
Adriatic Sea, Europe	43°N	15°E	33
Aegean Sea, Greece	35°N	25°E	31
Afghanistan, country in Asia	33°N	65°E	34
Alaska, Gulf of, North America	59°N	145°W	40
Albania, country in Europe	41°N	20°E	31
Algeria, country in Africa	25°N	0°	10
Andaman Sea, Indian Ocean	11°N	96°E	35
Andorra, country in Europe	43°N	2°E	32
Angola, country in Africa	12°S	18°E	12
Antigua and Barbuda, island country in Caribbean Sea	18°N	62°W	15
Arabian Sea, Indian Ocean	18°N	60°E	37
Arafura Sea, Southeast Asia	9°S	135°E	24
Aral Sea, Asia	45°N	60°E	28
Argentina, country in South America	40°S	68°W	17
Australia, continent and country	23°S	135°E	24
Austria, country in Europe	48°N	15°E	33
B			
Baffin Bay, North America	72°N	65°W	27
Bahamas, island country in Atlantic Ocean	25°N	78°W	15
Bahrain, country in Middle East	26°N	51°E	37
Baltic Sea, Europe	57°N	19°E	28
Bangladesh, country in Asia	23°N	90°E	35
Barbados, island country in Caribbean Sea	13°N	59°W	15
Barents Sea, Arctic Ocean	73°N	35°E	28
Beaufort Sea, Arctic Ocean	73°N	140°W	26
Belgium, country in Europe	51°N	5°E	32
Belize, country in Central America	17°N	89°W	14
Bellingshausen Sea, Antarctica	67°S	85°W	18
Bengal, Bay of, Indian Ocean	19°N	89°E	35
Benin, country in Africa	10°N	2°E	10

Bering Sea, Pacific Ocean	60°N	175°W	40
Bering Strait, Alaska, USA	65°N	169°W	40
Bhutan, country in Asia	27°N	90°E	35
Biscay, Bay of, Europe	45°N	5°W	32
Black Sea, Europe and Asia	43°N	35°E	28
Bolivia, country in South America	16°S	66°W	17
Bosnia and Herzegovina,			
country in Europe	44°N	18°E	31
Botswana, country in Africa	22°S	23°E	13
Brazil, country in South America	10°S	55°W	17
Brunei, country in Asia	5°N	115°E	23
Bulgaria, country in Europe	43°N	25°E	31
Burkina Faso, country in Africa	12°N	2°W	10
Burma, country in Asia	22°N	96°E	22
Burundi, country in Africa	3°S	30°E	13

C

Cabinda, district of Angola	5°S	12°E	12
California, Gulf of,			
Central America	29°N	110°W	14
Cambodia, country in Asia	13°N	105°E	22
Cameroon, country in Africa	5°N	12°E	11
Canada,			
country in North America	60°N	100°W	27
Cape Verde, country in Africa	16°N	24°W	10
Caribbean Sea, Central America	15°N	75°W	15
Caspian Sea, Europe and Asia	43°N	50°E	28
Celebes Sea, Southeast Asia	3°N	122°E	23
Central African Republic,			
country in Africa	6°N	20°E	11
Chad, country in Africa	15°N	20°E	11
Chile, country in South America	35°S	71°W	16
China, country in Asia	35°N	100°E	20
Colombia,			
country in South America	4°N	74°W	16
Commonwealth of Independent			
States, country in Europe and Asia	60°N	100°E	29
Comoros, island country in Africa	13°S	44°E	13
Congo, country in Africa	0°	16°E	12
Coral Sea, Pacific Ocean	15°S	160°E	25
Costa Rica,			
country in Central America	10°N	84°W	15
Croatia, country in Europe	46°N	16°E	31
Cuba, island country			
in Caribbean Sea	22°N	80°W	15
Cyprus, island country in			
Mediterranean Sea	5°N	33°E	36
Czechoslovakia, country in Europe	50°N	15°E	31

D

Davis Sea, Antarctica	65°S	90°E	19
Davis Strait, North America	55°N	59°W	27
Denmark Strait, Canada	66°N	25°W	27
Denmark, country in Europe	56°N	9°E	33
Djibouti, country in Africa	12°N	43°E	11

Dominica,			
island country in Caribbean Sea	15°N	61°W	15
Dominican Republic,			
island country in Caribbean Sea	19°N	70°W	15
Drake Passage, Antarctica	58°S	70°W	18

E

East China Sea, Asia	29°N	125°E	21
East Siberian Sea, Arctic Ocean	73°N	165°E	29
Ecuador, country in South America	2°S	78°W	16
Egypt, country in Africa	25°N	30°E	11
El Salvador,			
country in Central America	13°N	89°W	14
English Channel, Europe	50°N	1°W	32
Equatorial Guinea,			
country in Africa	2°N	10°E	12
Estonia, country in Europe and Asia	59°N	26°E	28
Ethiopia, country in Africa	10°N	40°E	11

F

Fiji,			
island country in Pacific Ocean	18°S	179°E	38
Finland, country in Europe	65°N	27°E	31
France, country in Europe	47°N	2°E	32
French Guiana, French			
department in South America	4°N	54°W	17

G

Gabon, country in Africa	0°	12°E	12
Gambia, country in Africa	13°N	16°W	10
Georgia, country in Asia	42°N	44°E	28
Germany, country in Europe	51°N	10°E	33
Ghana, country in Africa	8°N	1°W	10
Gibraltar, Strait of,			
Mediterranean Sea	38°N	5°W	10
Great Australian Bight, Australia	35°S	130°E	24
Greece, country in Europe	40°N	22°E	31
Grenada,			
island country in Caribbean Sea	12°N	62°W	15
Guatemala,			
country in Central America	15°N	90°W	14
Guinea, country in Africa	11°N	10°W	10
Guinea, Gulf of, Africa	3°N	4°E	10
Guinea-Bissau, country in Africa	12°N	15°W	10
Guyana, country in South America	6°N	59°W	17

H

Haiti,			
island country in Caribbean Sea	19°N	72°W	15
Hawaii, island in Pacific Ocean	20°N	155°W	39
Honduras,			
country in Central America	15°N	87°W	15
Hong Kong, UK colony in Asia	22°N	115°E	21
Hudson Bay, Canada	60°N	85°W	27
Hungary, country in Europe	47°N	18°E	31

I

Iceland, country in Europe	65°N	18°W	30
India, country in Asia	23°N	80°E	34
Indonesia, country in Asia	5°S	120°E	23
Iran, country in Middle East	32°N	54°E	37
Iraq, country in Middle East	32°N	44°E	36
Ireland, country in Europe	54°N	8°W	32
Israel, country in Middle East	31°N	35°E	36
Italy, country in Europe	43°N	12°E	33
Ivory Coast, country in Africa	7°N	5°W	10

J

Jamaica, island country in Caribbean Sea	18°N	78°W	15
Japan, country in Asia	35°N	139°E	21
Japan, Sea of, Asia	40°N	135°E	21
Java Sea, Southeast Asia	6°S	111°E	22
Jordan, country in Middle East	31°N	36°E	36

K

Kenya, country in Africa	0°	37°E	13
Kiribati, island country in Pacific Ocean	2°S	175°E	39
Kutch, Gulf of, Indian Ocean	22°N	70°E	34
Kuwait, country in Middle East	29°N	48°E	36

L

Labrador Sea, North America	57°N	58°W	27
Laos, country in Asia	18°N	102°E	22
Laptev Sea, Arctic Ocean	75°N	130°E	29
Latvia, country in Europe and Asia	57°N	24°E	28
Lebanon, country in Middle East	34°N	36°E	36
Lesotho, country in Africa	29°S	29°E	13
Liberia, country in Africa	6°N	10°W	10
Libya, country in Africa	25°N	18°E	11
Liechtenstein, country in Europe	47°N	9°E	33
Line Islands, Pacific Ocean	0°	160°W	39
Lithuania, country in Europe and Asia	55°N	24°E	28
London, capital of the United Kingdom	52°N	0°	32
Luxembourg, country in Europe	49°N	6°E	33

M

Mackenzie Bay, Antarctica	68°S	72°E	19
Madagascar, country in Africa	20°S	47°E	13
Malawi, country in Africa	12°S	34°E	13
Malaysia, country in Asia	5°N	102°E	23
Maldives, island country of Asia	4°N	73°E	34
Mali, country in Africa	17°N	0°	10
Malta, island country in Europe	36°N	14°E	33
Mannar, Gulf of, Indian Ocean	8°N	79°E	34
Mariana Trench, Pacific Ocean	12°N	146°W	38
Mauritania, country in Africa	20°N	10°W	10

Mauritius, island country in Africa	20°S	57°E	13
Mediterranean Sea, Europe	40°N	7°E	33
Melanesia, island group in Pacific Ocean	5°S	160°E	38
Mexico, country in Central America	25°N	105°W	14
Mexico, Gulf of, Central America	25°N	90°W	14
Micronesia, island group in Pacific Ocean	8°N	165°E	38
Monaco, principality in Europe	44°N	7°E	33
Mongolia, country in Asia	45°N	105°E	20
Morocco, country in Africa	33°N	8°W	10
Moscow, capital of Russian Federation, CIS	56°N	37°E	28
Mozambique, country in Africa	18°S	36°E	13
Mozambique Channel, southeast Africa	17°S	43°E	13

N

Namibia, country in Africa	23°S	18°E	12
Nauru, island country in Pacific Ocean	0°	166°W	38
Nepal, country in Asia	28°N	85°E	35
Netherlands, country in Europe	52°N	5°E	32
New Caledonia, island in Pacific Ocean	21°S	165°E	38
New York, city in United States	40°N	74°W	41
New Zealand, island country in Pacific Ocean	40°S	175°E	25
Nicaragua, country in Central America	12°N	85°W	15
Niger, country in Africa	16°N	10°E	11
Nigeria, country in Africa	10°N	8°E	10
North Korea, country in Asia	40°N	127°E	21
North Sea, Europe	56°N	3°E	32
Norway, country in Europe	62°N	10°E	31
Norwegian Sea, Europe	66°N	0°	31

O

Okhotsk, Sea of, Asia	55°N	150°E	29
Oman, country in Middle East	20°N	56°E	37
Oman, Gulf of, Middle East	25°N	58°E	37

P

Pakistan, country in Asia	30°N	70°E	34
Panama, country in Central America	8°N	80°W	15
Papua New Guinea, island country in Pacific Ocean	6°S	145°E	25
Papua, Gulf of, Papua New Guinea	10°S	145°E	38
Paraguay, country in South America	23°S	58°W	17
Persian Gulf, Middle East	27°N	52°E	37

Peru,			
country in South America	10°S	76°W	16
Philippines, country in Asia	12°N	123°E	23
Poland, country in Europe	52°N	20°E	31
Polynesia,			
island group in Pacific Ocean	5°S	150°W	39
Portugal, country in Europe	40°N	8°W	32
Puerto Rico,			
island in Caribbean Sea	18°N	66°W	15

Q

Qatar, country in Middle East	25°N	51°E	37

R

Red Sea, Middle East	20°N	38°E	36
Romania, country in Europe	45°N	25°E	31
Ross Ice Shelf, Antarctica	81°S	175°W	19
Ross Sea, Antarctica	75°S	165°W	18
Rwanda, country in Africa	2°S	30°E	13

S

Sahara, desert in Africa	23°N	5°E	10
St. Kitts and Nevis,			
island country in Caribbean Sea	17°N	63°W	15
St. Lucia,			
island country in Caribbean Sea	14°N	61°W	15
St.Vincent,			
island country in Caribbean Sea	13°N	61°W	15
San Marino, country in Europe	44°N	12°E	33
São Tomé and Príncipe,			
country in Africa	0°	7°E	12
Saudi Arabia,			
country in Middle East	25°N	45°E	36
Scotia Sea, Antarctica	58°S	45°W	18
Senegal, country in Africa	15°N	15°W	10
Seychelles,			
island country in Africa	5°S	54°E	13
Sierra Leone, country in Africa	9°N	8°W	10
Singapore, country in Asia	1°N	104°E	22
Slovenia, country in Europe	46°N	15°E	31
Solomon Islands,			
island country in Pacific Ocean	10°S	160°W	38
Solomon Sea, Pacific Ocean	10°S	154°E	38
Somalia, country in Africa	6°N	47°E	11
South Africa, country in Africa	30°S	25°E	13
South China Sea, Asia	13°N	115°E	23
South Korea, country in Asia	37°N	128°E	21
South Pole, Antarctica	90°S		19
Southern Ocean, Antarctica	63°S		18
Spain, country in Europe	40°N	5°W	32
Sri Lanka, country in Asia	8°N	81°E	34
Sudan, country in Africa	15°N	30°E	11
Suriname,			
country in South America	4°N	56°W	17
Swaziland, country in Africa	27°S	32°E	13

Sweden, country in Europe	65°N	15°E	31
Switzerland, country in Europe	47°N	8°E	33
Syria, country in Middle East	35°N	38°E	36

T

Taiwan, island country in Asia	23°N	121°E	21
Tanzania, country in Africa	5°S	35°E	13
Tasman Sea, Pacific Ocean	35°S	160°E	25
Thailand, country in Asia	15°N	102°E	22
Thailand, Gulf of, Asia	11°N	101°E	22
Togo, country in Africa	8°N	1°E	10
Tokyo, capital of Japan	36°N	140°E	21
Tonga,			
island country in Pacific Ocean	19°S	175°E	39
Trinidad and Tobago,			
island country in Caribbean Sea	11°N	61°W	15
Tunisia, country in Africa	34°N	10°E	10
Turkey, country in Europe and Asia	39°N	35°E	36
Tuvalu,			
island country in Pacific Ocean	8°S	178°W	38

U

Uganda, country in Africa	2°N	33°E	13
United Arab Emirates,			
country in Middle East	23°N	54°E	37
United States of America,			
country in North America	40°N	100°W	41
Uruguay, country in South America	36°S	56°W	17

V

Vanuatu,			
island country in Pacific Ocean	16°S	168°W	38
Venezuela, country in South America	7°N	66°W	17
Vietnam, country in Asia	15°N	105°E	22

W

Walvis Bay, southwest Africa	23°S	14°E	12
Weddell Sea, Antarctica	67°S	45°W	18
Western Sahara, country in Africa	23°N	13°W	10
Western Samoa,			
island country in Pacific Ocean	14°S	172°E	39

Y

Yellow Sea, Asia	35°N	124°E	21
Yemen, country in Middle East	15°N	47°E	36
Yugoslavia, country in Europe	44°N	20°E	31

Z

Zaire, country in Africa	2°S	24°E	13
Zambia, country in Africa	15°S	26°E	13
Zimbabwe, country in Africa	19°S	30°E	13

Scott E. Morris an associate professor of geography at the University of Idaho where his current areas of teaching and research interest include mountain geomorphology, field methods, and human impact on the landscape process. Dr. Morris received his Ph.D. from the University of Colorado, Boulder and is published prolifically on the formation and climatic history of mountain landscapes, the effects of wildfire and mineral resource extraction on soil erosion processes, and the influence of water diversion and channel modification on sediment transport.